TORRANCE PUBLIC LIBRARY

3 2111 015

S0-BXV-633

Katy Geissert
Civic Center Library
3301 Torrance Blvd.
Torrance, CA 90503

Slow News

WITHDRAWN

Other books by Peter Laufer

Organic: A Journalist's Quest to Discover the Truth Behind Food Labeling

The Elusive State of Jefferson

No Animals Were Harmed

Forbidden Creatures

The Dangerous World of Butterflies

¡Calexico!

Neon Nevada (with Sheila Swan Laufer)

Hope Is a Tattered Flag (with Markos Kounalakis)

Mission Rejected

Wetback Nation

Exodus to Berlin

Highlights of a Lowlife (editor)

Shock and Awe

Made in Mexico (illustrated by Susan L. Roth)

Wireless Etiquette

Safety and Security for Women Who Travel (with Sheila Swan Laufer)

Inside Talk Radio

A Question of Consent

When Hollywood Was Fun (with Gene Lester)

Nightmare Abroad

Iron Curtain Rising

070.43
L373

KGL

Slow News
A Manifesto for the Critical News Consumer

Peter Laufer

Oregon State University Press
Corvallis

The paper in this book meets the guidelines for permanence and durability of the Committee on Production Guidelines for Book Longevity of the Council on Library Resources and the minimum requirements of the American National Standard for Permanence of Paper for Printed Library Materials Z39.48-1984.

Library of Congress Cataloging-in-Publication Data
Laufer, Peter, 1950-
 [Slow news. English]
 Slow news : a manifesto for the critical news consumer / Peter Laufer.
-- First U.S. edition.
     pages cm
 "First published in Italy in 2011 by Alpha Test-Sironi Editore"--Title page verso.
 Heavily revised and updated translation of the Italian original.
 ISBN 978-0-87071-734-5 (alk. paper) -- ISBN 978-0-87071-735-2 (e-book)
1. Journalism. I. Title.
 PN4733.L3813 2014
 070.4'3--dc23
                        2013041304

Slow News: A Manifesto for the Critical News Consumer by Peter Laufer
Copyright © 2011 by Peter Laufer
Copyright © 2011 by Alpha Test S.r.L.
First published in Italy in 2011 by Alpha Test-Sironi Editore
First U.S. publication by Oregon State University Press in 2014
All rights reserved. Printed in the United States of America

Oregon State University Press
121 The Valley Library
Corvallis OR 97331-4501
541-737-3166 • fax 541-737-3170
www.osupress.oregonstate.edu

Contents

With love to Sheila

who questioned my priorities
whenever I drove our old Chevy pickup
17 miles across the Nevada desert
just to buy the latest edition
of the *San Francisco Chronicle*

Preface

Imagine summertime in Milan, and a leisurely lunch *al fresco* at the Villa Necchi Campiglio. I was meeting with Martha Fabbri, the publisher of the Italian edition of my book *The Dangerous World of Butterflies.* Later that day we were going to the Natural History Museum, where I was to talk about my experiences while researching the book.

But for now, the pasta was steaming and the wine was flowing. It wasn't quite a Fellini film, but we were enjoying the cinematic atmosphere we created (in fact, the venerable mansion itself stars in the film *I Am Love,* directed by Luca Guadagnino): an Italian-American literary lunch in the villa's quiet garden—an oasis in the noisy, crowded city. All we needed to complete the scene were over-sized movie star sunglasses and a Vespa or an Alfa Romeo to taxi us over to the public gardens.

Our talk drifted to the luxury of our luncheon. No television blasting in the courtyard competing for our attention, no *telefoninis* and their demanding rings. We weren't checking our Blackberries and our iPhones between courses.

Instead, prompted by the languid atmosphere, I mused to Martha about my nascent Slow News Movement, and the manifesto I was writing. "Yesterday's news tomorrow," I suggested, and Martha thought for just a moment, took a sip from her iced Cinzano or her pungent macchiato (at least that's what my Italian cliché-ridden imagination wants to remember), and announced that she wanted to publish this book.

Perfect.

It was, after all, Slow Food that inspired Slow News, and Carlo Petrini founded that compatible movement not far from where we were finishing our slow-motion meal. We agreed that the book should be launched in Italy, and in Italian. Where better to yell out, "Yesterday's news tomorrow!" than a land where the current political leader controled too much of the news media, where the lunches can linger for hours of Chianti and gossip, and where Julius Caesar is credited with founding that precursor to screaming tabloid headlines and incessant CNN droning, the *Acta*

Diurna—his daily news roundup distributed around the empire, complete with a sports section to divert the masses: the results of gladiator fights.

Martha and I closed the deal with a couple of Italian *baci* on the cheeks and an American handshake, and we ambled out of the villa into the frenetic streets of Milan with a book and a cause.

Introduction
Extra! Extra! Read All About It!

I'm sitting in a café, my iPad tossed over to the far side of the table while I write these words in a notebook I bought this morning for $2.99 at the local grocery store. With practiced strokes of my right hand, I'm making marks on the blue-lined white paper, using a Staedtler Mars Lumograph 100 pencil that rests with familiar comfort on my middle finger, held in place by my thumb and index finger. The Staedtler is filled with a 2B lead, a weight that softens as I write. Already my block letters are getting fatter and fatter. But as they thicken, the pencil slides across the paper with increasing ease, and the all-but-impossible-to-hear sound of pencil on paper gets even quieter. In fact, as I think about it, I'm not sure it's a sound of paper and pencil I hear over the ambient café clatter—it may just be the subtle vibration of the pencil on the paper that I perceive as a sound.

The pencil is about a third worn. The blue, black, and white paint on its six sides is worn, and raw wood shows through in places. When this one is worn down to a stub, I've got another in my satchel.

When the pencil point dulls, as it does now, I take a brief break from writing and sharpen the Staedtler. I use a heart-shaped blue plastic sharpener that I bought years ago in Mexico City for one peso. No batteries required. No moving parts. Just a blade held in place by a setscrew, so it's removable. The sharpening blade can be sharpened or replaced! The sides of the sharpener are scored, and I find myself feeling the sides of the plastic blue heart in my left hand and clicking my fingernails along the ridges as I scrawl these words with my right.

Okay, the Staedtler again is pin-prick sharp. The point scrapes against the paper for a few words until it—again—wears down a tad and flows on the paper like soft butter on bread. I look back on what I've written and I see my all-but-immediate rewrites: strike-outs, added words, arrows, and lines marking where changes were made minutes, even seconds, after the first draft was sketched into the notebook.

Meanwhile, my iPad sits on the table, dark. Its battery saver timed it off. Had I written this on its touch screen, I would see no handwritten history of my editing. My fingers would have been banging on its glass screen, not caressing my plastic heart (making me think of Mexico) and forming each letter as I see it appear on the heretofore-blank notebook paper, my poor penmanship a documented element of my personality. Were I writing this on my iPad, all I would be leaving besides the rapidly processed words would be my fingerprints on the glass. I would have been tempted often to check my email whenever I completed a thought rather than pausing to press the sharpening blade against the lead and the wood—a process that leaves me a moment to think instead of lusting after more incoming matter from the unending ping of my email inbox. Were I writing this on my iPad, I would have been chastised by Microsoft Word for misspellings, or for what Microsoft's programmers deemed were grammatical errors. I would have been tempted to Google "Chateau," the brand name embossed on my plastic heart pencil sharpener—a French brand name from Mexico, a romantic image for me that could have been Google-shattered with raw corporate data about pencil sharpener manufacturers.

I do not dismiss the utility of my iPad, word-processing programs, or Internet searches. On the contrary: I use them all the time. This is the first book that I've started to write by hand since 1988. But in the spirit of the idea that I would like to share through this manifesto, I'm setting aside the pixels for a moment and embracing the tactile value of slow handwriting— the luxury of taking time away from the seductions of computer-assisted writing to escape to this café with my notebook, pencil, and languishing still-dark iPad.

Writing by hand while the computer stays dark exemplifies what this book is all about. I am convinced that we need to learn how to slow down the hyperactive influences of news media on our lives. But this book is not an argument against the wonders of the technology revolution of our contemporary era. I embrace the potency of instant communication and of global Internet connectivity. Still, we need to recognize the frailties of innovations like the twenty-four-hour news cycle and so-called citizen journalists.

In this book I present what I consider the rules for a balanced and nutritious daily news diet, and launch my Slow News Movement, with its motto "Yesterday's News Tomorrow." Obviously its name is influenced by the Slow Food Movement. I want us to question the value of the perpetual fast-food-like empty-calories news that is processed to keep us addicted to it and instead consider that, for most news events, some time to ruminate is valuable for both the journalist in the field covering the story and the news consumer back home. And this book was inspired by Michael Pollan's *Food Rules*, a slim volume packed with sage advice, a compilation of wisdom from a journalist who specializes in what we eat and what it does to us. There are chapter titles like "Avoid foods that are pretending to be something they are not" and "Don't eat anything your great-grandmother wouldn't recognize as food." I realized as I was reading Pollan's book that there is an integral relationship connecting food and news. We must eat in order to survive. But accurate information can be another requirement for our survival. News reporting, I am convinced, vies with that other job as the world's oldest profession. In fact, I wager ours is the oldest. Customers seeking carnal diversion needed reporters for a question about the news critical to their quest: Where are the women?

Time to sharpen the Staedtler again.

Part One

On What News Is
& How It Is Made

Rule 1: Just the facts, ma'am

All news materializes immediately. As soon as it reaches you, no matter the mode it travels, no matter how long it takes to get to you, you grasp it immediately. A letter arrives and the stamp or the postmark or the return address of the sender announces its origin. Usually you know enough—the context is strong enough—that these indicators provide at least strong hints about the content. The news, even via an old-fashioned letter, starts immediately: whom it's from is quickly known. Tear open the envelope and scan the page. Key words like "killed," "I married," "money," spring out at you. Read the details just to fill in the blanks, but you get the gist of the news immediately.

E-mail can be even faster. A name or a place in the subject line and those receiving the message know something changed and it's probably not for the better. For example, if the subject line says, "Still no word from Johnny," the message probably is bad news. Good news too often is not considered news, but blessed routine.

The other day I was eating dinner in a restaurant with a colleague who is a crazed baseball fan. His favorite team is the New York Mets. Throughout the meal he was checking his mobile phone, not just for the score, but for developments as the game progressed. He has not purchased the service that allows him to watch the game live on his telephone. Instead, he receives messages that indicate things such as when a batter hits the ball. Then he must wait a minute or two before updated news comes to him about what occurred next. Did the batter get on first base or did the shortstop grab the grounder, fling it to first, and force the batter out? The news came to him delayed, which at least gave us a few undistracted minutes throughout the game to talk while we ate.

Whether it is a sports play, your cute little daughter's first ice cream cone all over her face, a revolution in Egypt, what your wife is cooking for dinner, or a bomb attack on the London Underground, news today travels to us almost as fast as it occurs—and sometimes instantaneously. Even if no journalist is present, passersby and participants in news events control technology to spread the word as the event happens.

So what's not the news in the post-Twitter world?

Before that question can be answered properly, there's an antecedent query. What's news?

Intriguing how close these two questions are: What's the news? What's not the news?

The news is anything that changes the status quo. (Although sometimes a status quo can be the news, as in the hopeful mantra, "No news is good news.") The glib definition that's served journalists for generations is: Dog bites man is not news, but man bites dog is news. The *Oxford English Dictionary* offers a broad definition: "The report or account of recent (especially important or interesting) events or occurrences, brought or coming to one as new information," and an elegant, poetic synonym: "tidings."

For the news to reach us, someone must report it. Think about the literally thousands of reporters who mass at events like Michael Jackson's funeral in 2009 or after disasters like the 2010 earthquake in Haiti, and the earthquake and tsunami a year later in Japan, or dramatic stories with inspirational endings like the 2010 rescue of the trapped Chilean miners. Most of those journalists reported essentially the same story, while around the world news was breaking and going unreported because there were no witnesses—professional or amateur—who chose to spread the word about what happened.

Is it the news if it occurs and it is not reported? Is it the news if what occurred is not in some database and available to the public? That's a question that concerned Italian journalist Tiziano Terzani, who noted in his investigation of Asian mysticism, *A Fortune-teller Told Me*, "There is one aspect of a reporter's job that never ceases to fascinate and disturb me: facts that go unreported do not exist." Making facts exist fueled his career and gave meaning to his own existence. "The idea that with every little description of a thing observed one can leave a seed in the soil of memory keeps me tied to my profession," he wrote.

Adding Terzani's premise to mine, the news is anything that changes the status quo and gets reported as the news. Nonetheless plenty of things change the status quo and—*Gott sei dank*—don't get reported as the news no matter how hard political propagandists, public relations agents, advertising artists, and others with ulterior motives may labor to get their clients' opinions and products into the headlines. Such orchestrated events, if not of consequential importance, with luck get shucked to the editing-room floors.

But there is another factor for the definition besides something that changes the status quo and gets reported as the news. We—the news consumers—are in partnership as never before with news reporters. The audience must agree that what happened is the news; otherwise, a variant of Tiziano Terzani's worry occurs. The news happens, it is reported, but no one pays attention to the change.

With this working definition of the news in place, what's not the news?

The news is not that which we already know. The news is not endless repetition of inconclusive elements of a news story that are of little relevance until a complete picture of that news can be reported. The news is not out-of-context factoids, pieces of information that tell no story but are just isolated pieces of information. What my son Michael calls "brain clutter."

Here's one of my favorite examples of a well-reported event that was not the news. A few days after the revolt began in Libya in February 2011 against Muammar Gaddafi, a ferryboat was loaded in Tripoli with American citizens and other foreigners wishing to leave the country. For a variety of reasons, the boat's departure was delayed for a couple of days. As the boat and its refugees approached the dock in Malta, CNN and Fox News both broadcast repeated live reports, their announcers standing on the dock, pointing to the approaching ferry, saying over and over again, "Here comes the boat, here comes the boat!" It was a script that changed only slightly once the boat had docked. The breathless reporters looked earnestly into their cameras and announced, "The boat is here, the boat is here!"

Of course television relies on dramatic pictures to tell news stories in a manner that practitioners hope will attract audiences. But these were not dramatic images. A ferry boat approaching a dock at night with a cargo of unknown Americans who chose to leave a country in turmoil maybe deserves a line or two—but not nonstop live coverage. And that's what my local newspaper gave it the next day. Under a photograph of the boat at dockside, the story simply read, "A ferry carrying 167 Americans and 118 other foreigners arrives at the harbor in Valletta, Malta, on Friday. The passengers were fleeing Libya's escalating turmoil."

So here's the Slow News rule: If it's going to be just a line in the back pages of tomorrow's newspaper, don't waste your time with the story in progress. All-news TV channels that linger on partial details and Internet news websites offering moment-by-moment updates of news story sidebars should be avoided or sampled with suspicion. There really are better things to do with our time than watching a ferryboat approach a Maltese dock. Go for a walk, draw a picture of the view out your kitchen window, practice the piano, re-read *War and Peace*.

My first journalistic trip to Korea forced me into the role of an enabler, a reporter perpetuating empty calories of news. It was 1983 and Ronald Reagan was president. I was an NBC news correspondent working out of the network's Washington, D.C., bureau. I was assigned to travel with the president and to report on what was a tightly choreographed journey. This trip to Asia was logged a few years before President Reagan made his famous "Mr. Gorbachev, tear down this wall!" speech on the west side of the Berlin Wall. The White House wanted a similar backdrop for us news reporters who were sending dispatches back to the States. Of course that meant a ride up Freedom Road to the DMZ. Camp Liberty Bell and Guard Post Collier were gussied up to impress the visiting Commander-in-Chief and watching world. The paint was fresh and the concertina wire was glistening. The Great Communicator made a typically appropriate speech to soldiers of the U.S. Army's 2nd Infantry Division on DMZ duty.

Looking north he said, "Communism is not the wave of the future and it never was—freedom is." With a nod to America's war in Vietnam he told the troops, "Yes, we, too, have our faults. But we've got a heck of a lot more to be proud of, and we're not afraid to say so." It was a good talk, as most of Reagan's speeches were, and reporters noted his remarks, and photographed him looking across the DMZ and speaking to the assembled soldiers.

Nothing wrong, of course, with reporting the news that President Reagan was at the DMZ. He was the first American president to do so, and Presidents Clinton, George W. Bush, and Obama all followed him to what Clinton called "the scariest place on Earth." But there was no need for so many of us journalists to follow Reagan around Asia, just as there was no need for news consumers around the world to be subjected to seeing the president's image—over and over and over again—holding binoculars while looking north and saying—over and over and over again on television screens and radio broadcasts worldwide—"Communism is not the wave of the future."

The idea behind the Slow News Movement certainly is not to ignore the news. That Ronald Reagan announced at the DMZ, "Communism is not the wave of the future," is an important historical footnote, still germane today. But imagine what other hidden news stories we could have uncovered and discovered had a majority of the horde of reporters who were tagging along on Reagan's tightly scripted trip broken away from the tour. Imagine what viewers, readers, and listeners could have learned about Korea—its history, culture, and contemporary society— had we international journalists been deployed elsewhere that day besides along the DMZ.

My own lasting memories of Korea are limited because the stopover I made with President Reagan was so brief: the highway to the DMZ lined with tank traps, the sparkling concertina wire at the 38th parallel north, a rushed shopping trip to a swank department store and its vast array of ginseng products, a store where I bought a vibrant silk outfit for my wife. Was it a *hanbok*? I can't remember and it's long gone from her clothes closet.

I want to take my own advice and return to Korea as a journalist practicing the Slow News doctrine. I want to study Korean history, culture and contemporary society—and then report, as the Slow News Movement motto preaches: "Yesterday's News Tomorrow."

News purveyors are increasingly skilled as carnival barkers, enticing us to keep connected with them while their advertisers try to sell products to us, products we likely did not realize we wanted until we were exposed to the clever and repetitive advertising. "Don't dismiss us" is the relentless message from the news companies. "Stick with us or you'll miss what's happening, and the details are coming soon, right after this commercial." Once the details eventually do come to us, we're told that there is more: further developments, analysis from "experts," speculation about what may happen next. We simply do not need most of this patter, and what we may need, we can learn at a pace we set for ourselves.

The BBC's Director-General Mark Thompson, before he decamped for the New World to take charge of the *New York Times,* in the introduction to the BBC's official policy book, proclaims that "in a perfect world the BBC Editorial Guidelines would consist of one sentence: use your best judgment." His recommendation was directed at his employees, but it is sound advice for news consumers. The BBC Editorial Guidelines go on for a couple of hundred pages of specific rules and regulations. Their goals are lofty and serve as another clear definition of news, from the point of view of a news purveyor. "We seek," says the Beeb about itself, "to establish the truth of what has happened and are committed to achieving due accuracy in all our output."

We news consumers need to consciously and carefully moderate our media—news and other media. I've experimented with writing letters in cursive with a fountain pen and sending them through the post. I try to avoid responding immediately to incoming email messages. I force myself to leave my mobile telephone in the car when I go out to eat in restaurants. I've closed my Facebook account, and I shut down my Twitter account after just a few "tweets." We need to decide for ourselves what media are worth our while, not just allow ourselves to be subjected to an endless barrage of unfiltered media assaults. We're in danger of missing the story because of the noise.

When I visited the Herman Hesse Museum in Switzerland, near Lugano, I lingered over the displays of his typewritten correspondence. Even were it salvaged and printed, it's difficult to imagine our contemporary email traffic as a compelling graphic exhibit. It all looks the same, and despite sophisticated digital storage facilities, it is all so perishable: the quartermasters at Facebook and Google can wipe it out with a few keystrokes. Let's write more with pen or pencil on paper and leave a lasting literary legacy of the personal news that happens to us.

Therefore, here's a second version of the first Slow News rule: Follow the advice of the veteran American journalist David Brinkley, who informed his public via an interview, "News is what I say it is; it's something worth knowing by my standards!" Decide for yourself what constitutes the news you can use. Don't waste your energy with the rest of what is promulgated as news. We don't have time for it.

Rule 2: Allow your news to stand the test of time

What news is important and why? Quasi-hysterical news presentations—especially on broadcast outlets—can lead readers, viewers, and listeners to believe that the information being foisted on them is critical to know (and to hear and see repeatedly), even though it may warrant only those few lines in the back pages of tomorrow's newspaper, like the ferry-to-Malta story.

Think about some of the important news stories you've lived through, and perhaps personally experienced. The 2001 attacks on the World Trade Center in New York, for example, or the fall of the Berlin Wall and the lifting of the Iron Curtain. The wars in Afghanistan and Iraq might be on your list, or the demise of Osama bin Laden in his Pakistan redoubt. How about the 1986 nuclear power plant disaster at Chernobyl, or—if you're old enough—the day Pope John Paul II was shot in St. Peter's Square or President Kennedy was assassinated in Dallas.

But even these history-making news events need not result in us punishing ourselves with a battering of repeated images and incomplete reporting. How many times was it necessary for you to see the footage of the airliners crashing into the Twin Towers and the victims jumping to their deaths? No question that viewing those pictures once is a requirement. We should feel the need to see the horrifying reality and our incredible technology allows those of us thousands of miles from such an event to view vivid images that might otherwise be difficult to imagine. A second time is understandable: it was such an unexpected and initially incomprehensible act that a second look helps us accommodate and accept the reality of the event. But looped over and over again?

Of course ratings-hungry CNN, and even the venerable BBC, replay such dramatic pictures. It is hard not to look at the flicker of the television even when something mundane and banal is broadcast. When the images are of human tragedy, it's extremely difficult to look away, no matter how many times we've seen them. Anomalous disasters captivate us. Television seeks ratings. Newspapers are in the business of selling the next edition.

Websites seek clicks that register usage and help sell advertising. When horrifying pictures keep us watching and reading, that's what will be printed, broadcast, and posted. Tabloids like *The National Enquirer* in the United States and *Bild* in Germany base much of their story choice on a simple formula: each article is designed to make the readers wish they experienced a life like the protagonist of the story or relieved that their own lives—as routine and boring as they may seem—are not consumed with the tragedies reported.

There is another reason for the repetition of words and pictures, particularly on all-news television broadcasts. Especially early in the development of a breaking news story, reporters and editors suffer from a limited supply of information. So that first draft of history being reported is repeated to fill the news hole until more detailed words and pictures are available to explain what happened and why, and what it may mean to your personal life.

In this case the Slow News rule is simple, if hard to enforce: Unless the earthquake or war is in your own backyard, when news breaks sample those initial reports and reject the repetition. It is a rare news story that is so important to your immediate existence that you need to know moment-by-moment whatever the news outlet does (or does not) know. Check in with a radio newscast every few hours at most, look at one cycle of an all-news TV channel once or twice a day. Read a news website with the same frequency your grandparents read the newspaper—daily, not hourly. Reject the option for news "alerts" to be delivered to your allegedly smart phone, such as the urgent email from the *New York Times* to my wife that read, "N.H.L. and Players Union Reach Tentative Agreement." Hockey labor relations updates can wait until tomorrow's sports page, thanks just the same. Don't make the default page of your browser a news site; a museum makes a comforting alternative, as does the tourist bureau of a dream vacation spot.

"First reports are always wrong," is the considered opinion from Victoria Clarke about dispatches from war zones. She served President George W. Bush as a Pentagon spokeswoman. "It's a fundamental truth in military affairs," she said. Add that it's a fundamental truth regarding most breaking news. "In most of what it does, continuous real-time broadcast news is a failed experiment," wrote author James Gleick in *New York* magazine after watching the debacles featured on TV as the medium struggled with the Boston Marathon bombings story. Arrests were reported when none had been made, suspects were reported identified when the police had none. Later Maureen Dowd interviewed social critic Gleick for her *New York Times* column and he told her, "Reporters doing TV news in real time are an oxymoron. You can't gather news and present it at the same time. Part of newsgathering is the gathering part." Skipping that critical newsgathering step reduces reporters to rumor mongers.

Except for those who lived nearby in Connecticut or knew the victims and their families, there was no need for anyone to subject themselves to moment-by-moment (and often erroneous) updates about the Newtown elementary school massacre.

The non-news presented as news is even more important to tune out. Did you know Princess Diana personally? Probably not. So, unless you've really got nothing better to do with your life, why is it necessary to be barraged with miniscule details and speculations about the car crash that killed her? Again, don't blame the news media. They're doing their job: selling papers and building audiences.

"If it bleeds, it leads," we in the news business tend to say about story placement, because that's what attracts attention from the audience. Broadcasters fill television screens and radio speakers with macabre tales that usually matter directly only to the victims and their friends and families. But our lives should be full enough that we don't need to wallow in the misery of anonymous others. Car crashes, murders, and celebrity divorces are the sorts of stories that might be worth a footnote in our common curriculum of the daily news, but we should spare ourselves the gory details of these common occurrences, especially when they are repetitive and superficial.

Another version of the second Slow News rule: Before investing time with a new news story, consider its importance to your life. Make the news you choose stand the test of time unless, of course, you use your news mostly as entertainment.

Rule 3: Question news that offers superficial, minimalistic, and incomplete information based on incomplete reporting

The job of the news report is to help the news consumer understand events and their nuances. Quick and easy answers to social quandaries usually spell propaganda, not news.

Be wary of the glib and the incomplete. Earthquakes and other natural disasters offer a good example. Inevitably after a consequential jolt of an earthquake the initial reports will offer something along the lines of, "An earthquake centered near [insert city name] woke residents early this morning. There are no reports of damage or injury." There may well be no reports of damage or injury because reporters have not yet arrived in the city or managed to get in contact with places where there was damage or injury. These first reports often are followed by updates adding damage reports and casualty figures, reports and figures that increase as journalists arrive on the scene and rescue workers report back to their headquarters.

When the infamous bomb blew in the midst of the government district in Oslo in the summer of 2011, initial reports—whether via tweets, on Facebook walls or old-fashioned telephone calls from an eyewitness to a colleague—were fragments. Even hours after the devastation, Oistein Mjarum, communications chief for the Norwegian Red Cross, whose offices were close to the epicenter of explosion, was careful when he told the BBC, "We have never had a terrorist attack like this in Norway, if that is what it is." His caveat showed appropriate concern. He was waiting for verification of his visceral response to the devastation.

Some of the initial news reports after the Oklahoma City federal building was bombed in 1995 suggested foreigners were to blame for the terrorism. "A Beirut-style car bombing," said *The Wall Street Journal*. A police all-points bulletin that was quoted by reporters described suspects with "Middle Eastern appearance" and "dark hair and beards." The bomber was homegrown, and as all-American looking as the proverbial mom and apple pie.

Another prime example is the coverage of the 2012 Newtown school shootings. Initial reports "confirmed" that there was more than one shooter; those early reports also incorrectly identified the murderer, and called his mother a school employee. It is extremely difficult to avoid paying rapt attention to such an anomalous and horrific story as it breaks. When the shooting started I was driving from Los Angeles to the Mojave Desert. I was listening to a jazz radio station, enjoying the sublime Southern California landscape when I heard the first reports of the tragedy. I struggled against my human (and journalist's) instincts to switch frequencies to KNX, the CBS all-news station, testing my ability to embrace the Slow News Movement. I forced myself to stick with the jazz. No question I would check back later in the day to learn what more was going on in Newtown. But I found no value in subjecting myself to the often incomplete and erroneous moment-by-moment developments. I'm sure if I had followed the adrenaline-pumping updates as I cruised across the desert to Joshua Tree, I would have arrived mighty depressed and not necessarily better informed.

Even for a story with as much significance (and as thoroughly managed) as the assault by U.S. armed forces against the Osama bin Laden hideout in Pakistan it was unnecessary to stay glued to the TV after the initial report of his death and the official explanation made from the White House by President Obama. Immediately after that announcement, news outlets began disseminating a barrage of contradicting reports regarding what had occurred in Pakistan. Writing in *Slate* magazine just a day after the raid, media critic Jack Shafer compiled a list of inconclusive and contradictory reports from the world's premiere newsgathering organizations. The American Web-based news source *Politico*, Shafer reported, implied that two helicopters took part in the raid. The London *Telegraph*, he wrote, reported that one of four helicopters involved had crashed and burned after it was "apparently hit by fire from the ground," and that the helicopters were mustered for the raid at a base in Pakistan. He quoted *The Wall Street Journal* citing an unnamed official as informing the paper that "two helicopters took part in the operations," and that "one Pakistani helicopter involved in the raid crashed after it was hit by firing from the militants." *Time* magazine, wrote Shafer, counted four helicopters at work, and reported that a malfunctioning CH-47 chopper was destroyed at the scene, while *The Atlantic* identified the aircraft as MH-60s. *The New York Times* quoted eyewitnesses that "spotted three helicopters."

That there are conflicting reports published during the first hours after a secret story of global interest breaks is understandable. Reporters are scrambling to find credible sources who will provide them with details. The sources may well have ulterior motives when they decide to inform reporters—from spotlighting their own perceived self-importance, to cozying up to reporters in hopes that a favor now will result in a favorable story in the future, to attempting to put the perpetrators of the news event in a good (or bad) light, to spreading misinformation as part of a coverup, to honestly trying to help inform the public.

As news consumers, we need to remember that we should be deciding for ourselves what we need and want to know, and when. Less than twenty-four hours after the announced bin Laden raid, does it really matter to most of us what type and how many helicopters of what nation's armed forces were used to attack him? If we're curious about the details of the operation, why not wait until the official version along with any thorough contradictory and credible conflicting investigations are published. What's the hurry?

Here's the third Slow News rule: Make sure your news spaghetti includes some meatballs (or tofu). That means avoiding the simplistic, the superficial, and the jingoistic unless—again—you're just seeking news-oriented entertainment.

Rule 4: Don't avoid news and commentary that you disagree with

Turn on the radio anywhere in America and you can hear an outpouring of shrill voices: talk radio "hosts" ranting and raving, interacting with the audience via telephone. The impact of these shows and the power of their stars is well dramatized in the 1988 Oliver Stone film *Talk Radio*, based on the Eric Bogosian stage play of the same name. The talk radio phenomenon is not limited to America; it's spreading rapidly throughout much of the world.

But in Italy, as in many other countries, talk radio is not as strident as it is in the U.S. Two of the most popular shows that Italian commuters listen to are broadcast during the evening rush hour: *Zapping*, hosted by Aldo Forbice on Rai Radio1, and *La Zanzara*, an increasingly entertainment-oriented show hosted on Radio 24-II Sole 24 Ore by Giuseppe Cruciani. These programs are influential—European Parliament member Mario Borghezio was suspended from his party, Lega Nord, after an interview at *La Zanzara* during which he expressed sympathy for the ideology behind the far-right terrorist attack in Oslo—but normally milder compared to American commercial-laden talk radio. The Italian hosts, even when narcissistic, usually present moderate viewpoints. When they act dogmatic their opinions are diluted or counteracted by co-hosts. Nonetheless, disputes between the audience and the egocentric hosts are common on both programs, which—of course—drives ratings ever higher.

Are these egomaniacal announcers (and their participating listeners) in the U.S., Italy, and elsewhere examples of free speech at work? Are they demagogues abusing the public airwaves for personal and political gain? Are they tools of radio station owners interested only in maximizing profits?

Radio is so commonplace we often relate to it as a utility; like gas and electricity it's always available. But unlike heat and light, radio content influences society from a tribune of presumed credibility. Consequently, it is critical for us to be aware when radio is misused for manipulation.

Credible opinion polls from the Gallup organization and the Pew Research Center for the People and the Press warn us that a substantive number of Americans claim talk radio as a primary source of their news information. Today talk radio in the U.S. is powerful and dangerous. Hate mongers, propagandists, and disinformation specialists rule American talk radio. They yell lies and play a harsh divisive role in society. Empowered by a deregulated and consolidated radio industry, these talk show hosts, often sporting no credential other than a gift of gab, believe their own rhetoric and revel in their own sense of self-importance. Instead of being ignored, or at least ridiculed, they are revered by a susceptible audience. These self-appointed loudmouths are sought after for their alleged news expertise, but rather than accuracy, fairness, and clarity, most of them tend to broadcast self-aggrandizing bombast.

An example of the damage this degenerated kind of talk radio hosts can cause society came up during a conversation I engaged in with California State Senator Gil Cedillo about drivers licenses for undocumented immigrants, while I was researching a book about immigration (*Wetback Nation*). Cedillo couldn't separate talk radio from the immigration debate. He worried about the potency of right-wing talk radio to perpetuate fear and hate against migrants. The hypocrisy frustrated him. "Thousands of people are dying," he said about immigrants trying to cross the border from Mexico into California. "Should they survive, we're happy to have them take care of our kids, take care of our parents, pick over 90 percent of the foods in the Central Valley. If you really don't want immigrants here, stop using them. I guarantee you, whether you're eating Moroccan food or Chinese food or Italian food, in the best restaurants in Beverly Hills or San Francisco or Carmel, there are Mexicans out there making it in the kitchen.

"In those cars," he told me about California's commuter culture and its radios, "starting at three o'clock, there's some buffoon who is just blaming every problem that they have on immigrants. The white working class is frustrated," he explained. "We're into this generation where the children are not going to do better for the first time than the parents."

"They're not just frustrated," I said. "They're scared."

"They're scared," he agreed. "Precisely."

"They're scared of other people."

"Yes, and it's fueled by this phenomenon of AM radio," he said about the talk shows that blanket California's airwaves. "Shock jocks who pretend to be serious thinkers play a major role." He shook his head, sad with his own frustration. Years after we talked, legislation authorizing driver licenses for all drivers who pass the California driving test no matter their immigration status finally was approved by the California legislature and signed by Governor Jerry Brown.

Yet, from the left-leaning *Huffington Post* to the hard-right *The Wall Street Journal* editorial page, from the carnival-like right-wing Fox "News" to the Communist party line *China Daily*, from the UK's liberal *Guardian* to rive gauche *Le Monde* in Paris, it's important for news consumers to know the other sides of the story—interpretations that differ from our own.

The vast majority of the listeners to *The Rush Limbaugh Show*, broadcast on too many radio stations, are middle-aged white men who identify themselves as "conservatives." Limbaugh spews his news-based propagandistic programming out over the national airwaves for three hours a day, five days a week. His audience is huge and there is no question that his diatribes influence American politics. When he urges his followers to lobby their representatives in Washington, politicians' offices on Capitol Hill are flooded with email advice and complaints.

Those of us who may take issue with Limbaugh's worldview need to be familiar with his interpretations of the news, with the misinformation and disinformation he disseminates, and with the opinions he articulates— opinions that infect too many of his followers. The very fact that they call themselves (without irony and at his urging) "Ditto Heads" when they speak on his radio show is a clear indication of his influence over too many millions of Americans.

Distasteful as it may be for those who disagree with Limbaugh, it is critical to hear him use the public airwaves to say things such as, "How can America be Islamophobic? We elected Obama, didn't we? If this is a nation that is Islamophobic, how do we elect a man whose name is Barack Hussein Obama?" Or, "You have either Obama and the Democrats or America. You can't have both." Spoken via the de facto authority that comes with a radio transmission, combined with Limbaugh's news announcer inflections, the repetitive attacks ultimately turn into truisms for too many of those millions of listeners.

We should spend at least a few minutes every few weeks consuming opinions about the news contrary to our own, even if it is a difficult chore. One student of mine, when assigned to listen to another radio talk program, the self-aggrandizing eponymous *Glenn Beck Show*, wrote at the close of his research paper about the experience, "At the same time as I was having my intelligence insulted, I was bored to tears. Please, don't make me do this again." It was an understandable response, perhaps, but nonetheless an important assignment. How else would this university student be aware that each week millions of radio listeners were hearing Beck proclaim things about President Obama like, "This president, I think, has exposed himself as a guy, over and over again, who has a deep-seated hatred for white people or the white culture." The next day he reiterated his stance, saying, "I think the president is a racist."

Does Glenn Beck have an influence on his audience? At the end of August in 2010, on the anniversary of the "I Have a Dream" speech by Martin Luther King, he managed to get enough of his listeners and viewers to come to his "Restore America" march and rally in Washington and jam the Mall in front of the Lincoln Memorial. There he and Sarah Palin, reported the *Washington Post*, "called on the nation to recommit itself to traditional values he said were hallmarks of its exceptional past." Knowing the words that create such a powerful force is critical to understanding the power of those words. And the assignment to consume opinion with which you disagree is not an issue of the right versus the left, nor is it limited to the propaganda of any one nation.

In Italy it was easy for opponents of Silvio Berlusconi's policies to find news reports to disagree with. The former prime minister's company, Mediaset, controls three of the nation's four private television channels; and, indirectly, during his tenure as Italy's political leader, he controlled the three state TV outlets because he chose the channels' news managers. This in a country where most political news reaches voters via broadcast media.

Germans interested in understanding the mindset of three million or so ethnic Turks living in their midst likely would profit from studying reports of the speech Turkey's prime minister Recep Tayyip Erdogan gave when he visited Düsseldorf. "They call you guest workers, foreigners, or German Turks," Erdogan told a cheering crowd. "It doesn't matter what they all call you. You are my fellow citizens, you are my people, you are my friends, you are my brothers and sisters. You are part of Germany, but you are also part of our great Turkey." Americans who are interested in another viewpoint of what the Muslim world thinks about the U.S. military—besides that of American reporters—could profit from spending some time reading and watching the work of Al Jazeera.

Here's the Slow News rule: Seek reportage you disagree with and study it; learn what others believe and what they use as news sources.

Rule 5: Trust accuracy over time

"It must be so because I read it in the newspaper" are not words to live by. Rely on news outlets and news sources that have proved themselves to you to be reliable. This simple rule is the corollary to seeking news and commentary from points of view other than your own. A journalist has no stock in trade other than credibility. No amount of advertising, self-promotion, bragging, or other hyperbole can compensate for losing the trust of the audience. And that trust is built up over time.

A proven technique for finding news outlets that you can trust is to consume a wide variety of news that deals with two types of subjects: news that you know about in detail from personal experience and news that is completely obscure to you.

Pick a news story you witnessed or were part of or that you otherwise have studied enough so that you feel confident that you understand most of its aspects and subtleties, its characters and locales. Next choose newspapers and broadcasters, bloggers and magazines, the whole array of news peddlers, and immerse yourself in the stories they present about what occurred. It's best to do this exercise over time with a few sample news stories. But you likely will find, after testing just one story, that there are a few outlets with which you feel comfortable regarding how that story you know was presented to the public. Those periodicals and broadcasters should become your A List of where to turn when you want to know what's happening in the news.

A second device for finding your primary news sources is to choose a handful of stories you're not familiar with—stories that interest you but you've not experienced or studied. Do the same drill. Expose yourself to a wide variety of reporting and stick with those you feel did a better than average job of explaining a new issue to you and that stand the test of time and variety. Make sure these outlets continue to satisfy your news needs over time and the ever-changing news of the world.

Consider the report in *Parade* magazine that Springfield, Oregon, offers the most strip clubs per resident of any city in the United States.

Springfield lies just across the Willamette River from Eugene, home of the University of Oregon, where I teach. So I read the *Parade* story with mild amusement, especially since I've noticed a few seedy-looking establishments in Springfield soliciting passersby to come on in and see girls shed their clothes.

A few days after the *Parade* story ran nationwide (the publication claims a weekly circulation of over thirty-two million; it is an insert in newspapers from coast to coast and border to border), Niel Laudati, the community relations manager for Springfield, insisted the story was patently false, and he impugned *Parade's* journalistic integrity for promulgating a false impression of his city. *Parade* acknowledged that it had based its story on a report by a magazine called *Exotic*, a report that was reiterated in the Portland, Oregon, weekly newspaper *Mercury* (which calls itself "Portland's Most Awesome Weekly Newspaper"). Check out the *Exotic* website for yourself; it's hard to imagine that you would rely on it as a credible source for assessing a city's commercial offerings. *Parade* did not bother to do its own reporting, a job that could have been done with a few well-placed telephone calls. And although *Parade* admitted its error when queried by offended Springfield boosters, it did not bother to tell its own readers about the mistake in the next issue of the magazine. "We regret not double-checking before publication with the Springfield mayor's office, which brought this error to our attention," was the official statement from *Parade's* editor, Maggie Murphy. "We apologize and want to set the record straight." *The Mercury*, showing a flair for entertaining corrections, embraced the controversy with panache and announced, "Attention! Springfield, Oregon, is a Nice Place to Raise a Family and NOT the National Strip Club Capital."

"It's not very helpful," Springfield booster Niel Laudati said about the negative image the *Parade* story constructed about Springfield. "Before you do this to a city, at least check it out." Laudati's words offer good guidance for all of us as we decide what to believe in a news report: check it out. Even had *Parade* run a correction in its pages, apologies rarely wield the impact of the original incorrect story. Headlines screaming gross errors do not fade from memory because of a few lines of correction in the back pages of a paper or at the end of a broadcast. We tend to remember the first (loud!) impression.

The *Guardian* offers a "Corrections and clarifications" column that can make for some amusing reading. The paper apologized for reporting that a U.S. military squad "killed Obama." A simple typesetting error. Or perhaps it was a mistake caused by a joker in the print shop. Another *Guardian* error could have ruined wine, cheese, and bread picnics along the Seine for readers who failed to note the paper's mea culpa. "A report on a Paris competition for best baguette," wrote the editor, "gave the weight for submitted loaves as between 240 g and 310 g, and then went on to quote the president of the bakers' union as saying the salt content should not exceed 18 g. To clarify: that was per kilo of flour. Meaning that in a 250 g loaf the salt would be about 4.5 g or just under a teaspoon." Whew!

The Wall Street Journal files its mistakes in a column titled "Corrections and amplifications." The business newspaper made a whopper when it listed the first-quarter losses for a company at $1.47 billion. The unfortunate subject of the article only lost one and a half million U.S. dollars that quarter.

The column "*Interventi e repliche*" (Statements and Replies) in the Italian *Corriere della Sera* offers readers the opportunity to respond to articles they find unjust or inaccurate. These comments often are followed by a reply from the journalist who originally wrote the piece and is quite candid about admitting the paper's sins. Perhaps the most original corrections column in the Italian press is published in the weekly magazine *Vanity Fair*. Its name is "*Ufficio accuratezza*" (Accuracy Office) and it invites readers to point out any "wrong names, dates that seem incorrect, imprecisions, topics to analyze in greater detail" they may find in the magazine. Fact checking as well as typos: a rare attention to formal accuracy in the contemporary press landscape.

These correction columns try to make amends for mistakes that may be inevitable or inadvertent, but we need to set a threshold for judging news outlets.

So this is the Slow News rule: Rely on news outlets and news sources that have proved themselves to you to be reliable.

Rule 6: Embrace fairness in news reports

There is no such thing as objective reporting; all journalists come to their stories from distinct points of view. But a subjective report can be, and ought to be, fair.

"Just the facts, ma'am, just the facts," was the standard line Sergeant Joe Friday is credited with demanding as he interrogated witnesses to crimes portrayed on the old *Dragnet* radio and television series. But what are the facts? Facts are elusive. Our memories play tricks on us. We may well believe we know for sure exactly what happened during an experience we share with others, but each of us will offer a distinctly different variation on the theme if we are asked to tell the story of what occurred.

Try it some time as a parlor game.

Gather all the guests at a party, except for one, in a room. At an appointed time cue the one left out to barge into the room and make some sort of a scene. He or she can run into the room and jump up and down saying something silly and then run out again. Or rejoin the group, walk up to a woman, and hug her and kiss her. Or come into the room, light a cigarette, and then tickle a friend. It makes no difference what he or she does. It just must be something unexpected and brief. Then he or she must exit the room.

Next, one by one and in a separate room, ask the guests to explain what happened. Or pass out paper for the guests to note their versions of what occurred. Each will tell a different story. Perhaps the overall description of events will be similar, but as soon as two or more people gather, they will tell two or more versions of any event, even something simple that they have experienced first hand together. It cannot be otherwise because we all interpret events via our own personal prejudices, philosophies, and experiences.

In addition, no matter how recent were the events that occurred to us and around us, our memories are subjective. We humans are not perfect recording machines. Some of what we see, hear, feel, touch, smell, etc., we retain. But we're constantly editing. We don't notice some of what surrounds us. Other elements of what happens we jettison, deciding—usually subconsciously—that it is not of great enough importance to register. Other stuff, and this often irritates and frustrates us, we simply forget. Try as we may, we cannot remember what we may think is a crucial aspect of a story. It's lost to us.

These same human realities and frailties plague journalists. That is why it is ludicrous to pretend to be an objective reporter. There is no such thing as objectivity in journalism. It may be an impossible goal worth striving for, but even as a goal, objectivity is a false god. We journalists come to the stories we cover laden with the baggage of our lives, and that is a good thing. But our life histories make even an attempt at objectivity a mirage. Every story we report is influenced by what's happened throughout our lives.

The same is true for the entire process of journalism, from story choice through to placement in a periodical or a broadcast, on a website, or flashed as a tweet. Why are events in Libya worth more space in an Italian newspaper than similar events in Yemen? Because of the intertwined histories of Libya and Italy, of course. But that is a subjective decision. What is going on in Yemen is, naturally, probably of more importance to the Yeminis, or even to Italians interested in Yemen, than what is happening in Libya. The editor makes a subjective choice.

Reporters make subjective choices as they pick and choose what to write about events they witness—and how to tell the story. A good example is the article Robert Fisk crafted for the London *Independent* after NATO's commanders decided to send a missile into the Belgrade studios of Radio Televizija Srbije, killing several of the broadcaster's employees. Fisk described the carnage in its grotesque detail yet he made clear he was no fan of the broadcaster's programming. "Yes," he wrote, "Serbian television could be hateful, biased, bad. It was owned by the government." He described rescue efforts and NATO's rationale for the attack on what it called Serbia's "propaganda machine." But he did not shy from a reporter's analysis. "Once you kill people because you don't like what they say," he concluded in his report, "you have changed the rules of war."

As news consumers, we need to forget about objectivity and instead seek fairness, clarity, and accuracy in the news reports we choose. Fairness means treating credible opposing viewpoints with respect. Without fairness, the news simply is propaganda. It may be interesting and even of value to know about, but it fails the test for a daily news diet. Without accuracy, or at least a concerted attempt at achieving accuracy, a news report becomes misinformation or disinformation. And without clarity, we're forced to wade through a waste of our time. A meandering and confused news report, especially in today's era of perpetual information overload, is not worth our time.

The Slow News rule is: Forget objectivity; search for reporting that is fair, accurate, and clear.

Rule 7: Treat "former journalists" with skepticism

Fired after a stellar career at CBS News because a report questioning President George W. Bush's military credentials was flawed, Dan Rather quickly resurfaced with his own news program on the cable television channel HDNet, a venue tiny by comparison with CBS. But HDNet offered him the opportunity to continue reporting regularly for his own TV news magazine. Once a journalist, always a journalist. He explained his disinterest in retiring to a rocking chair with a line all journalists would recognize, "I love doing the news." And he dismissed the importance of audience size in a *Mother Jones* magazine story about what motivates him as a journalist. "I'd go door to door telling people the news."

Consider this headline from *The Washington Post*: "Jay Carney, former journalist, is named White House press secretary." The story explains that Mr. Carney's professional career began as a reporter, that he became the *Time* magazine Washington bureau chief, and then worked as "communications director" for Vice President Biden before signing on to handle his former colleagues for President Obama. He doesn't necessarily call himself an ex-journalist; that's the title used by the *Post* headline writer. But it is unimaginable that Mr. Carney—with his experience as a Washington reporter himself—won't be keeping notes during his White House tenure for a book about his experiences inside the presidential bubble. Storytelling must be in his blood in order for him to be a *Time* bureau chief and to do the job of spinning the official version of President Obama's day-to-day affairs.

The *Post* headline writer can't decide Jay Carney—or any other journalist—is an ex-journalist just because he's taken a job outside of the profession. But if Mr. Carney does write that book or returns to reporting breaking news it's worth wondering if his dedication to his duties (and the personalities) at the White House will influence his reporting.

Once a journalist, always a journalist.

What's problematic is when the journalists wander through revolving workplace doors that can taint their journalism by association. "Former journalist signs PR contract with Bahrain," was the headline in *Roll Call*, the Washington newspaper that specializes in Capitol Hill politics. The story reports that Christopher Cooper, who left *The Wall Street Journal* in 2009 to become a public relations agent, was selling his PR services to the Bahraini government after its soldiers attacked civilian protesters demonstrating in Manama's Pearl Square. American law required Cooper to announce his deal to the Justice Department and sign up as a foreign agent. His initial contract, worth $20,000, explained his role as providing counsel that "may include outreach to reporters in an effort to explain various positions held by the government of Bahrain." Does this business deal mean that Christopher Cooper is a former journalist? Cooper worked at the New Orleans *Times-Picayune* before joining *The Wall Street Journal*. He is the co-author of a well-reviewed book, *Disaster: Hurricane Katrina and the Failure of Homeland Security*. His LinkedIn biography lauds his twenty years in journalism and his reporting from over fifty different countries. Does his contract with, as he's described it on LinkedIn, "a foreign government seeking help in dealing with an internal crisis" mean he is a former journalist? Should the fact that he chose to take a job flacking for an authoritarian government make his readers question the veracity of his twenty years reporting from fifty countries? Or is it the government of Bahrain that should be cautious, and worried that his journalism instincts will kick in while he is on their payroll, resulting in stories he would not otherwise have had access to and they would not want to see reported?

Winston Wood was a longtime editor at *The Wall Street Journal* and tried to dissuade others from the journalist's life in a column he wrote for the *Columbia Journalism Review*. Citing the collapse of traditional journalism business models, Wood preached, "If you're interested in journalism, even now, give it a shot. It's a great way to learn about the world, develop communication and analytical skills, and provide a public service. But over the long haul, there's more stability and better money to be made panhandling." That questionable conclusion doesn't hide the fact that he was still a journalist as he deplored its current status, reporting on the status of the industry that formerly employed him.

Along with self-proclaimed ex-journalists, question credentialed journalists. Who provided the credentials and what—if any—sacrifices were made when those formal papers were accepted? Beware of news that comes to you from government-licensed journalists. Yemen, Nicaragua, and Zimbabwe are just three examples of where it is illegal to practice journalism without a government license. So-called syndicates operate throughout the Arab world in concert with governments and they certify who is authorized to report the news.

In some circumstances, corporate filters join with governments to determine which professionals may call themselves journalists. In Chile, the title of "journalist" is reserved by law for those who graduate from an officially recognized journalism school. In Italy, to be a *professionista* journalist requires a long apprenticeship or a degree from a journalism school followed by an oral and written examination. But aspiring journalists in that country can follow a separate path from the official "professional" route, becoming a *pubblicista* after they have published a certain number of pieces. And anyone who convinces an Italian editor to accept their work can get published, even if they don't have any official title; hence the titles are mere indicators of status and social privileges, not the sole arbiters of journalism opportunities.

In reality, each journalist decides if he or she is a journalist. Of course there are pragmatic reasons—necessities—to accommodate restrictions in some societies in order to gain access to newsmakers and news events (and to survive as a journalist), but news consumers should exercise an extra dose of informed skepticism when news comes from officially sanctioned reporters. A couple of the appropriate questions to ask in such cases are: What reporters are kept out of the official journalism club, and why?

Even in countries with laws guaranteeing free and independent news media, there are de facto licensing issues. In the United States, for example, several state governments have enacted shield laws that protect journalists from being forced to disclose their news sources. If journalists decide for themselves who is a journalist—if anyone can be a journalist who wants to be—does that mean any citizen can hide behind the shield laws? The answer is no. Courts decide who is entitled to shield law protection, and it is a particularly controversial and difficult ruling to make in this era when we all can own the equivalent of a printing press and a broadcast station with just a laptop and a broadband Internet connection.

A state legislator in Michigan tried in 2010—without success—to convince his colleagues to pass a law that offered journalists working in Michigan the opportunity to carry a government-issued journalism license. State Senator Bruce Patterson wanted applicants to show a journalism degree, proof of three years professional experience, and three writing samples, and be of "good moral character." Senator Patterson argued that such a system would help citizens know which reporters to trust. "What's the definition of a reporter?" asked the senator. "I haven't been able to find out? What's a reporter? What's a journalist? I thought you had to have a degree in journalism but apparently not. I could retire and be a journalist."

Exactly.

Perhaps the most entertaining example of how there are no former journalists comes from *The Front Page*, the play (made into films) written by Chicago newspapermen Ben Hecht and Charles MacArthur. In the movie directed by Billy Wilder, there is a scene where Walter Matthau, a star reporter's boss, meets the reporter's fiancée (a young Susan Sarandon). The reporter, played by Jack Lemmon, has quit his job to move from Chicago to Philadelphia; he's decided to trade his reporter's notebook for the life of an advertising copywriter. His boss doesn't want to lose him and he explains to the fiancée that a news reporter would make a no-good husband.

"Marry an undertaker," he says, "marry a blackjack dealer, marry a pickpocket, but never marry a newspaper man."

"That's why I'm making him quit," she asserts.

He rejects the possibility. "You can't make a leopard change his spots or hitch a fire horse to a milk wagon. And he'll be like a fish out of water."

The Slow News rule: Once a journalist, always a journalist. Be wary of those who claim otherwise.

**Rule 8: Choose your experts well
and shut the TV off when the anchorman
knows no more than you do**

Avoid those who self identify as black-journalist, or gay-journalist, or Vietnamese-American-journalist; they just may harbor an agenda besides reporting the news. A journalist is a journalist is a journalist. That a reporter may be black or French or one-armed or Catholic is not of primary importance to their coverage of the news, even if they decide to specialize in black, French, one-armed, or Catholic issues. But to suggest with a modifier that a journalist's status is overtly and perpetually inflected by race, ethnicity, national origin, sexual preference, religion, etc., etc., is a bright caution flag for the audience.

"Anything that compromises our independence hurts the credibility of the product, and credibility is the lifeblood of journalism," wrote editor Mike Clark in the Jacksonville (Florida) *Times-Union*. "I cannot be a hyphenated journalist," he explained. "My only obligation is to readers of the *Times-Union*, defined in the broadest way possible."

Watch out for what the Italians call the *tuttologi*, those journalists who claim to be instant experts whatever the latest headline. These self-proclaimed "experts" may be encouraged to call themselves experts because the title is freely adopted in other contexts. The National Federation of the Italian Press, in its labor negotiations with the Italian Federation of Newspaper Publishers, seized the modifier to create a new professional category. An Italian journalist is assigned the "expert" title after eight years of service (and spending five years as an "expert" results in promotion to the position of a "senior journalist").

There are, of course, some extraordinary expert journalists: experts in a region or a discipline or a specific beat. Although no discipline requires an expert journalist, a reporter with a medical degree may well be in a better position to explain a disease than a general assignment reporter with experience only on the police beat. It is those instant experts who are problematic.

Robert Fisk, no matter what you may think about his stated points of view (no attempts at objectivity in his work), knows the Middle East better than most reporters. The London *Independent* Middle East correspondent, Fisk has been immersed in the region since he moved there in 1976 from his native England.

Fisk is an expert worth reading.

J. Jesús Blancornelas knew more about Mexican drug traffickers and their infiltration of government than most reporters; he specialized in coverage of the Mexican drug wars. The co-founder of the Tijuana newspaper *Zeta*, Blancornelas experienced the story firsthand: He was the victim of assassins who tried to silence him in 1997 when they blocked his car in Tijuana traffic and pumped over a hundred bullets into it, four of which hit him. His bodyguard was killed and he spent months recovering before returning to work. When I interviewed Jesús Blancornelas at his heavily guarded office I asked him if he and *Zeta* were role models for journalists. "No, no, no, no," he insisted. "There are no role models except the truth. The truth is the role model."

Blancornelas was an expert worth reading (he died of cancer in 2006).

For the better part of last century's second half, if you wanted to read about sports in Italy, Gianni Brera was an expert worth reading. His specialty was soccer. Drawing from mythology and literature, from foreign languages and regional dialects, from the memory of teams and players that he knew inside and out, and from his thorough technical knowledge, he reinvented Italian sports jargon. Brera took pleasure in writing about gastronomy in addition to sports, but he did that with some sense of humor and never considered himself a *tuttologo*, the faux-expert type of journalist that should be avoided.

Tuttologi are not to be confused with general assignment reporters. Invaluable journeymen know a little about almost everything, and they are experts at being a quick study. They can learn a little background about a breaking story in a hurry, and create a first draft of history about the breaking news. But this wise preliminary work on a developing news story is not to be confused with the vacuum that often fills radio and TV newscasts. Don't waste your time with reports that tease you with worthless information about something that is about to happen. Just wait for it to happen and you'll know what it is. The goal of the tease is to keep you connected to the medium in question; television is expert at trying to convince its audience not to look away from the screen because if you do you'll miss something crucial. It is a ridiculous thing to argue because television always replays, replays, and replays breaking news immediately after it breaks.

A textbook example occurred when American news anchors filled time during special live reports prior to President Obama's announcement that Osama bin Laden had been killed in Pakistan by the U.S. military. Reporters were told by the White House to expect the Obama speech, but they were not told of its contents. On Fox News, the tease-and-fill commentary by anchor Geraldo Rivera typified a reporter trying to keep an audience watching despite the fact that Rivera had no clue what the president was about to say to the world. Mediabistro.com compiled representative clips of Rivera's act as the world waited for the president's speech.

"The White House is saying that President Obama will be making an extraordinary statement," he told viewers, calling the statement, "highly unusual. Whatever the matter is," he mused as he filled broadcast time, "we don't know." He speculated about the speech "perhaps concerning events over the last twenty-four hours in Libya." Looking with concern at the camera he added, "It may have to do with the terrible series of storms." Severe tornados had just caused death and destruction across the southeast United States.

"So do you want to opine?" journalist Rivera asked a colleague, identified as a Fox News military analyst, who joined him on the Fox News set.

"Well, I think it's a national security issue," intoned the analyst, with the concerned and serious look of an expert. "It could have something to do with what's going on in Libya, I think it may very well be that, or it could be in Syria. We don't know."

Exactly. They don't know. So why watch until either the president starts talking or they do know? Especially with the tools we have today to alert us of breaking news—a flash on a mobile phone, for example, or an alert on our computer home page—why waste time with this drivel, which continued, of course.

Geraldo Rivera acknowledged the inanity of his broadcast during the wait. He looked at the camera and pleaded, "Please, ladies and gentlemen, forgive my rampant speculation, but this does bring to mind the words, 'We got him,' meaning they had captured Saddam Hussein." And then, "We do not have any indication except for our surmise that it has something to do with Libya."

At that the "military analyst" announced, "I think it has something to do with Colonel Gaddafi, perhaps his demise."

"It would be death or war, it seems to me," Rivera continued the conjuring, "or an awful terror plot." At that point he might have realized how distant he was from reporting the news and he added, "and again I don't want to scare people at home," another somber and concerned look at the camera, "but ladies and gentlemen, this is what it is."

Right. And it is a wait for an announcement. Why waste time with the Fox News bantering? It is clearly no more valuable than speculating with your friends and family at home. Why not spare yourself the inanity of the broadcast and just wait to hear from the primary source: Obama?

On the TV, Rivera is still thinking Libya. "I want very much to know exactly when the last time anyone saw Muammar Gaddafi alive was."

This sputtering is not so much an indictment of Geraldo Rivera's act that night as it is a recommendation that we do not bother watching the talking heads fill airtime. Imagine the challenge of his job: broadcast to the nation when he has nothing to report. Given that assignment, his performance is admirable—but as theater, not news. "This is a big, bad world," he tells his viewers. "It could be anywhere."

"It could be something in Korea," offers the analyst.

"Let's say what we know it is not," announces Rivera. "It is not a nuclear attack. Were it that there would be seismological proof because such an attack would be literally earth shaking."

The Fox News screen is split, showing the White House at night, and White House correspondent Mike Evans, who reports to Rivera about the impending Obama announcement, "It's not clear if it will be about Gaddafi or some other foreign policy matter elsewhere in this crazy world."

"It is a crazy world, Mike," agrees the anchorman.

Suddenly Geraldo Rivera has an internal news flash, which he shares with America and the watching world. "Hold it!" he exclaims. "Ladies and gentlemen, something I just thought of! What if it's Osama bin Laden? Wouldn't that make our weekend?" He smiles. "How that son of a bitch has wrecked our lives. Wouldn't that be a wonderful way to cap a weekend?"

After that exclamation comes a disclaimer. "These are not facts." He looks at the camera again. "I am not reporting anything to you. I'm just saying [the news analyst] and I will be high five-ing and the tears will be flowing if the news is that good." Then he looks around the studio. It seems likely at this point that he's received a credible report about what the President is about to announce. "We think," he says, and repeats, "we think," and then looks around the studio again asking his colleagues, "What do we think?"

After the long wait and repeated fantasizing, Geraldo Rivera obtains confirmation and proclaims, "Osama bin Laden is dead! Happy days! Happy days, everybody! This is the greatest night of my career!"

The Slow News rule: Avoid "hyphenated" journalists and know-it-alls.

Rule 9: Avoid echo chamber reporting

All journalism is investigative. If what is purported to be a news report is not investigative, it is merely clerical work.

The New Republic's critic Stanley Kauffmann famously said about Truman Capote's *In Cold Blood*, "This isn't writing, it's research." He was wrong, of course, but it was a witty paraphrase of a famous claim against the work of Jack Kerouac by Capote: "This isn't writing, it's typing." These exchanges of insults make me think about stories presented as news that aren't.

Remember in this era of Facebook and Twitter that Facebook updates and tweets from newsmakers are not news. They may be information, but that's not news. News, since we were cavemen drawing on our cave walls, requires an intermediary: the journalist. If the caveman who whacked the mammoth came home and scrawled his own experience on his cave wall, that was autobiography. If another caveman was along on the hunt, watched the kill, came home, and recorded what he saw on the wall, that was journalism. Sometimes the newsmaker and the journalist can be one and the same, but that requires both a rare news event and rare reporting talent.

As for non-news, the worst offenders are news organizations that print or broadcast verbatim announcements from public relations agencies. There is nothing wrong with accepting material from PR functionaries as background for stories. But to stuff such propaganda as is into the news pages or a newscast is scandalous, the scandal made more egregious only by those print and broadcast businesses who completely prostitute themselves and sell the opportunity for self-promoters to appear as if they and their causes (usually commercial) were legitimate news.

Almost as bad are the lazy reporters and editors who accept information without checking it and without advancing the story by reporting further developments. Crime statistics from the police are examples. Earnings reports from a company are others. An account of a battle by the military of one side of the conflict is still another example.

That's not journalism, that's stenography—without at least verification, it's just stenography. All news reporting should be investigative reporting. The latter term is redundant.

There is a difference between information dumping and knowledge building. In today's heavily mediated world we're awash with information. We can Google anything and find factoids. We're bombarded with information via the Internet and our mobile phones and other so-called New Media even while the relics of Old Media continue to thrive: books, for just one example.

The Slow News rule is to seek information that builds knowledge. Thorough reporting about important world news developments or about news that interests us or about news that is particularly crucial to our lives builds knowledge, makes us smarter, better citizens, and makes us much more fun to hang out with.

Beware of the Big Story Syndrome. When mobs of reporters flock to one story the result is needless repetition. Think about the hordes of writers and photographers waiting for the Chilean miners to come out of the bowels of the earth alive and well in October 2010. It was a thrilling positive news story, of course, full of human pathos and redemption. But think also of all the news stories that were going unreported or underreported worldwide all those days the miners were underground because of the resources that were shipped to Chile.

When the world's attention is riveted on one Big Story, it's a good time to troll obscure news outlets to find intriguing news pushed from the front pages by the Big Story.

Skillful media manipulators know how to take advantage of distraction. That's why governments and businesses tend to announce bad news when few are paying attention. Saturday afternoon is a good choice for obscurity. The weekday news reading/watching/listening routine is disrupted by the leisure of the weekend. The audience is at the beach or at the theater or sleeping late. The bad news slips with ease quickly into the ether, reported but often undigested. In 2011, for example, on the afternoon of Saturday, August 13 (which in Italy is more of a Saturday than any other because it is smack in the middle of the summer holiday period), the appointments of presidents and commissioners of the Italian public research agencies were announced on the Ministry of Education's website. The editor of the Italian edition of *Scientific American*, Marco Cattaneo, called this choice for a date *"carboneria,"* that is, "it looks like the news was meant to be kept hidden."

The Big Story Syndrome can distract the public just as thoroughly as a premeditated maneuver to hide bad news on the weekend. Seek news that teaches something new.

The Slow News rule: All journalism worth your while should be investigative journalism, and sometimes it must be actively sought.

Part Two

**Who Are the Media
& What Are the Sources?**

Rule 10: Shut off the all-news channels whenever you can

We news consumers are conditioned to flick on the TV news and let the so-called twenty-four-hour news cycle dictate the interpretation of a day's events to us. But we can break that habit, without losing touch with the common curriculum of news shared with friends and neighbors.

Take breaks from the assault of nonstop news. Just because all news radio stations offer "all news all the time" does not mean you must listen to "traffic and weather together" every ten minutes. Just because newspapers perpetually update their websites doesn't mean you must keep reloading the homepage, follow their tweets, and note their smart phone app alerts and read their email updates.

I just bought today's *San Francisco Chronicle*, my hometown newspaper. It costs a dollar these days. It's almost noon. That means most of the news in this newspaper is going to be yesterday's, or the day before yesterday's: *Yesterday's news tomorrow!* My Slow News motto.

I hold the paper and enjoy the feel of its pages and the smell of the ink as I explore the printed photographs, all while sipping a leisurely cup of tea. The texture of the images is different from their pixilated cousins glowing on my iPad when I read the *Chronicle* on its website, sfgate.com. As I look at the headlines and read those stories that interest me further than just a glance at the headlines, I see nothing I needed to know yesterday. I didn't need a bulletin flashed to me announcing that a National Institute on Drug Abuse study was released, a study that concluded teenage marijuana use is increasing (the subject of one of the articles in this issue). There was no urgency in my learning that census results indicate black and white Americans are choosing to integrate.

A prime example of yesterday's news tomorrow is a debate reported in this paper, a story buried deep on page three of the third section. The article is about a proposal to reduce automobile traffic in San Francisco and raise needed revenue for the city by charging a toll for each car that crosses into the city limits from adjacent San Mateo County. Yesterday I heard the story reported on the all-news radio station in San Francisco, KCBS. The announcer sounded more than excited, the delivery was quasi-frantic. The radio report included excerpts of speeches by lawmakers. The politicians from San Mateo County were decrying the arrogant elitism of the San Francisco policymakers. The lawmakers from San Francisco were bloviating about crowded streets and city debt. The story was repeated throughout the day on the radio, relentlessly. But by the close of business at city hall, the idea was dismissed as a non-starter.

Non-news.

When I saw the truncated story deep in the newspaper, I could dismiss it with a glance at the headline, a headline that announced in a small typeface: "San Francisco Supervisors Back Away from 'Southern Gateway' Toll."

The Slow News technique for dealing with breaking-news hysteria blasting out of your car radio is a simple one. Switch the channel from the all-news station to a music station. Even though it can be compelling to listen to the breathless announcer tease upcoming stories, change the station. You rarely need to hear the play-by-play of the day's news assaulting you from the car's speakers. It's not a baseball game. Or be daring! Shut off the radio and enjoy the quiet. Contemplate. Meditate. Every few hours check in with the news station for a summary of events if you really fear you may miss something important to you.

Such an exercise—checking the news every few hours—is not necessary. In today's overmediated societies, you can relax with your favorite music or in silence, confident that if there is an earthquake, war, or vital celebrity divorce someone nearby will find out in an instant via their iPhone, Twitter feed, or a Google alert, and they'll feel compelled to tell you immediately. Then you can switch over to the all-news station for details about something you choose to learn about rather than just being a passive consumer of news noise packaged to make it sound important.

Ration your television news viewing time: CNN, BBC, Al Jazeera, and other TV news assaults. Yes, the pictures of some breaking news stories are important cultural artifacts to share. But in general the news consumers' time is best spent with other-than-television news sources.

Wean yourself from the perpetual drone of CNN and its all-news cousins, from their repetitive and superficial treatment of what they consider is the news. CNN is seductively addictive, especially when there is breaking international news—war, political turmoil, or natural disasters, for typical examples. Give us a juicy scandal like Tiger Woods and his so-called sex addiction or the South Carolina governor ditching his wife for a South American rendezvous with his Argentine mistress or the ongoing post-Arab Spring turmoil and it's easy to slip into the Laz-E-Boy for endless updates. Sometimes there are those iconic pictures and sounds that are important to see and hear. One time. Or maybe twice. Remember the images of the World Trade Center buildings under attack or Katrina-flooded New Orleans or even of some royal wedding. But more often than not CNN and the others repeat the same few seconds loop of misery or weirdness over and over and over again; it's input we can do without, and which unnecessarily add to our understandable upset about the state of our poor world.

When I talked about the Slow News Movement on the Oregon Public Broadcasting radio show "Think Out Loud," Portland psychologist Ruth Parvin sent an email to the show explaining that she often prescribes "news-free days" to her patients to combat anxiety and depression. "I believe that the more primitive part of the brain reacts to each repetition of a murder, fire, or other awful thing as though it is a new event," she theorized. "If we hear about the same shooting fifteen times a day, that does not count as simply one event but somehow alerts the nervous system every single time we hear it."

Of course there are exceptions to this rule. There are times when a report on CNN or its competition provides a neat package that thoroughly brings us up to date on something important that we previously knew too little about. CNN shows its pedigree at times of disaster, when it dedicates its resources to the one breaking story. Such coverage to many viewers is a reminder of the story that established the network's international fame—the first Gulf War. CNN's brave correspondents remained in Iraq after the bombing of Baghdad began, their reports narrating images that are iconic for our era: the yellow tracers criss-crossing the city's night sky, and the sky itself turned an unnatural sickly green once it arrived on living-room screens around the world. But such instances are few indeed and rarely worth the waste of time spent wading through the vacuous pabulum that endlessly precedes and follows those moments of valuable cable TV news.

We're conditioned by broadcasters to think that we need to know what is going on as it is going on. That's rarely the case. And in the rush to immediacy, CNN's reporters and their competitors' often shove material on the air before they know what it means, and long before they can interpret the events with any depth or consequence. A Tom Tomorrow cartoon on my office wall sums up the problem. A TV news talking head says, "Welcome to Short Attention Span News! Here's a picture of the president! It looks like something's happening in another country! Well, that's all for today! Tune in again tomorrow—for as much news as we think you need to know!"

Once safely ensconced in the White House, President Obama lashed out at "a twenty-four-hour news cycle where what gets you on the news is controversy. What gets you on the news is the extreme statement. The easiest way to get fifteen minutes on the news, or your fifteen minutes of fame, is to be rude." He's correct. Those rude remarks are repeated incessantly, repackaged with usually vacuous "updates" designed to keep you in front of the tube. Be rude or do something shocking or be a victim of a disaster or crime. The media-savvy president is a master television craftsman, but in today's breaking news marketplace, where noise often trumps ideas, he's challenged trying to compete with the rude and the shocking.

The instant availability of perpetual newscasting makes CNN an easy diversion from what haunts us. Syndicated columnist David Sirota, a fellow at the progressive think tank Campaign for America's Future, believes that scandal "gets us to turn on the television, tune in to the latest manufactured drama, and drop out of the real battle for the republic's future." He's correct, too. How empty or burdened are our own lives if we can be titillated continuously by the indiscretions of others? Better to take a walk with the dog than to watch one more time as another apologetic politician or athlete descends from hero to zero in front of the cameras.

Yet it is easy to be a victim of the box. We can rationalize flicking on the BBC, CNN, or even Fox News for a fix of what's supposedly important; there may be something happening that's important to know. (Fox News, of course, for the satisfaction of not only a hit of news, but also as a reminder of how perverse its version of its slogan "Fair and balanced" continues to be.) So what to do? How to follow the Slow News dictum that you shut off the all-news television channels whenever you can?

The first step is to realize that most of what's fed to us on the all-news TV channels can be a gleaned from a quick glance at a newspaper or a website devoted to the news. You can prove this to yourself with a simple exercise. With a pad of paper, a pencil, and a stopwatch, tune in for an hour of CNN or its equivalent. In a column, note the time spent watching commercials and promotional announcements for other shows on the channel. In another column note how much time is spent promoting upcoming stories on the show you've tuned in to watch. Finally, keep a count of how many stories are broadcast during that hour and how much of the hour is used telling you vital details about those stories. I promise you that you'll be shocked by how little time is devoted to what passes for news coverage and by how few stories are covered during the hour even though their treatment is minimalist.

Now, using the same amount of time occupied by those few stories during your sample TV hour, look through a newspaper—any decent daily. Or do the same exercise with the website of a newspaper or a news aggregator (CNN's website included), no matter their political point of view. I guarantee you'll pump more information into your brain faster when you're far from the churning TV talking heads. In addition, you get the obvious advantage of deciding for yourself which story to read past the headlines and how much detail you want about each story.

Credible professional surveys suggest the above exercise will teach you that you're not learning much in return for all the hours spent watching the news channels. According to a study by the Pew Research Center for the People and the Press, "The coaxial and digital revolutions and attendant changes in news audience behaviors have had little impact on how much Americans know about national and international affairs." Some fifteen hundred Americans nationwide were asked questions about current affairs, a sample that Pew called representative. The study concludes, "On average, today's citizens are about as able to name their leaders, and are about as aware of major news events, as was the public nearly twenty years ago." Not that the scores of citizen awareness were much to write home about—an example: only about three quarters of those polled by Pew could name the vice president of the United States.

Some newspapers responded to the twenty-four-hour news cycle by creating a new editorial position: the continuous news editor. As domestic correspondent for what *The New York Times* calls its Continuous News Desk, David Stout explained his role. "We are always trying to balance speed and accuracy," he told readers of the brand. "My job is to write a quicker, and therefore less detailed version of an article . . . than will appear in the following day's newspaper. I think there is a need for both kind of articles in this day of twenty-four-hour news."

Not that the transition to digital and its various platforms is so easy to carry out in a system that was designed in the era of hot-lead type created by hulking Linotype machines. In September 2010, *Corriere della Sera*'s editor-in-chief, Ferruccio de Bortoli, wrote a letter to his colleagues at the paper explaining how, given the deep and fast changes in the industry, "all the agreements and business practices that have hitherto governed our industrial relations no longer make sense." According to de Bortoli, it was unacceptable that part of the editorial staff refused to work on the Web or demanded special remuneration for it and was reluctant to engage in training programs for the new technologies. They welcomed the success of the paper's Web TV with suspicion, the editor said, and he noted that the iPad edition did not include the contribution of any journalists from the paper edition. The harsh tone of the letter caused a two-day strike and started a labor dispute between the editor-in-chief, the editorial board, and the publisher. In February 2011, according to the editorial board, "the wall dividing paper staff and Web staff remained intact."

Of course the transition to digital continues, bringing radical changes to the media business. David Stout may be right, the *Times* may need to protect its flanks from bloggers and serve its subscribers with credible news reports generated at a blogger's fast pace. But that doesn't mean we need to pay attention 24/7. There is news that we need to know immediately—reports of threats to our welfare, like bombs exploding in downtown Boston. And then there is news that can wait until reporters corroborate it and ensure that it is correct; for example reports of arrests for the Boston Marathon bombings.

The Slow News rule: Don't pay attention just because the TV and radio and newspaper are all yelling, "Pay attention!" The Fox News slogan is, "We report, you decide." The Slow News slogan is, "You decide whether to pay attention to what they report."

Rule 11: Know your sources

Who says the news you're consuming is "fair and balanced" (the Newspeak slogan from Fox News)? It is critical to be aware of the personal and professional backgrounds of the reporters providing information to you, along with the corporate allegiances of the companies employing them and directing their newsgathering activities. Skillful masking of conflicts of interest can be exposed with some basic research. Who owns what news media and why is a critical question for news consumers.

The Italian media landscape is a fine example. Well known to many is that Silvio Berlusconi owns an abundance of the country's news-producing companies (and indirectly controlled government-owned news outlets in his position as a prime minister). Did those news outlets treat the longtime prime minister with proverbial kid gloves? *Mama mia!* Of course they did. Berlusconi's family media holdings include television, film, and music production, magazines and newspapers and books, advertising agencies, and printing plants. Even a soccer club—AC Milan is among his other holdings—can be used as a propaganda tool. *"Forza Italia"* (Go Italy) is what Berlusconi named the political party he founded and when he announced in late 1993 he would run for the next elections it was with a sporting metaphor: *"discesa in campo"* (entering the field).

A variation of the kid gloves theme occurred when *The Wall Street Journal* "interviewed" Rupert Murdoch in 2011 as the *News of the World* phone-hacking scandal was escalating in the UK. The paper's questioner tossed one softball after another at the press lord who, as most readers of the venerable newspaper know, owns *The Wall Street Journal*. His company, said Murdoch, handled the crisis "extremely well in every way possible" and just made "minor mistakes." The paper's advisory board acknowledged—days later—that its reporter should have engaged in "tougher questioning" of the boss. But that advisory board is just that. It exerts no control over the paper's reporting, editing, and subsequent content.

Rupert Murdoch's holdings blanket the Anglo-Saxon world. An incredible number of local television stations across America are Murdoch owned, not just the infamous Fox News. His TV empire extends across Africa, Asia, and Latin America. What may be a surprise to many viewers is that Murdoch holds a majority interest in the fabled National Geographic television brand. The HarperCollins publishing imprints are his with branches in the United States, Canada, the UK, Australia, New Zealand, and India. His newspaper chain was founded in Australia and now circumnavigates the world. The bawdy *News of the World* in the UK was a Murdoch production until he sacrificed it in an attempt to defuse the phone-hacking scandal, but so is that legendary British broadsheet, *The Times* of London. He bought *The Wall Street Journal* to serve as a relatively staid and respected counterpoint to his tabloid *New York Post* (famous for its attention-grabbing headlines like the typical screamer, "HEADLESS BODY IN TOPLESS BAR").

Just down the highway a few hours from my new hometown, Eugene, Murdoch owned the *Daily Tidings* in bucolic little Ashland, Oregon, a university city of just twenty thousand souls. In Eugene, the *Register-Guard* is still owned by the Baker family ("A newspaper is a CITIZEN OF ITS COMMUNITY" the *Register-Guard* yells from its masthead). Alton Baker was the publisher from 1927 until 1961. Alton Baker III is the current editor and publisher. On sunny days I take walks downtown, along the Willamette River, in Alton Baker Park. The Baker family probably influences its paper's news coverage more than Murdoch influenced the *Daily Tidings'* coverage of Ashland. He's busy elsewhere and the Bakers live in Eugene. So disinterested was Murdoch in Ashland that, in fact, he sold its newspaper in 2013 to another out-of-town investor. It is important to know who owns what.

Again, as we know from Rule 6, there is no such a thing as objectivity in news reporting; objectivity is impossible. Journalists, editors, and other media people bring our personal prejudices to all aspects of news production. What stories we choose to report is where the subjectivity starts. Where we place them in the paper or the broadcast is subjective and influenced by a number of factors: what we think is important, what we ourselves find interesting, how many papers we think the story will help sell. Of course our own prejudices influence the reporting and writing of stories. We cannot, as journalists, separate ourselves from our work. Our emotions, our life experiences, our priorities for society—none of these human traits can be excised from our journalism.

What we can do—rather than worship that false god of objectivity—is strive for journalistic sainthood in disciplines where our aspirations can easily become reality. Clarity is a good place to start. If a story is clear and easily understood, we're serving our public. Fairness is crucial. If we accept the impossibility of objectivity, we had better embrace fairness. As we saw in Rule 6, fairness means treating credible opposing viewpoints with respect. For clarity and fairness to play their appointed roles, a third replacement for objectivity is needed, and that is accuracy. If a news reporter's work passes the clarity, fairness, and accuracy tests, then his or her point of view only enhances the story. If we news consumers know the prejudices of the reporter, we can add the story to our curriculum of knowledge relatively free of worry that we're being propagandized against our will.

Point of view need not be political; it can be artistic. Consider the image that adorned the front page of the *San Francisco Chronicle* on September 1, 2006. It was an exquisite photograph of a soldier leaving his girlfriend for Iraq, shot by Darryl Bush.

Bush's extraordinary snap is a spectacular example of the type photographer Henri Cartier-Bresson characterized as capturing a "decisive moment." But as used by the *Chronicle*, an image that in other contexts could be art or simply news reportage becomes, to my sensitivities, pornographic. If a qualifier is appropriate, call it military-porn. That it was published just days before the fifth anniversary of the attacks on the World Trade Center and the Pentagon only adds to the propagandistic value of the photograph.

The image is an extraordinarily poignant and dramatic photograph of a soldier leaving for war. It completely dominates the paper's front page, and it is framed so that, when the paper sits in a sales box, all you see above the fold is the caption in upper-case letters: A KISS FOR THE ROAD, and a fatigues-clad torso leaning out of a bus window. When you open the paper and spread it out to its full broadsheet size, the full-color picture explodes with an emotionally wrenching storyline used through the ages to summon men to war.

Above the shirt pocket on the fatigues are the words, "U.S. Marines." The soldier's head—reaching far out the window—sports its military buzz cut, and a pair of dark sunglasses protects him. Reaching up to him is that paragon of American womanhood: a statuesque blonde. Their lips are just touching, precisely outlined. She's just seventeen, according to the story, he's a sturdy nineteen, and off for his training in the California desert before deployment to Iraq.

It is a gorgeous photograph. It is beautifully erotic, and perfectly composed, and mind-numbingly depressing. Its message is blatant: war = glory = sex. It is pornographic not because of its sex appeal, but because of the impact it makes as an illustration covering a newspaper's front page, exacerbated by its headline: A KISS FOR THE ROAD. Its sex appeal is inexorably linked to war, and—because of the timing of its publication—not just with the Iraq War, but also with the George W. Bush Administration's cynical attempts to continue to merge the Iraq War with the 9/11 attacks five years prior to the publication. The use of the Darryl Bush (no relation to the president as far as I know) photo was a nice tool for the U.S. military, then struggling to line up new recruits—even if all the *Chronicle* was trying to do was sell more papers.

Be wary of being subconsciously influenced by a photograph. No anti-war editorial or sobering reportage from the front can compete with the graphic potency of that lithesome California beach blonde, barely clothed, giving herself up to a G.I. Joe with "a kiss for the road." It is a seductive picture, and it screamed out of newsstands across California, while bodies in flag-draped coffins were being shipped from Iraq to Dover Air Force Base in Delaware, a site where *Chronicle* photographer Darryl Bush would not be allowed to practice his extraordinarily fine skills with a camera because during the Bush presidency photographers were banned from shooting pictures of the arriving Iraq War casualties.

At the height of the first President Bush's Gulf War, I was working at a radio station in San Francisco when another reporter walked into the station's newsroom and looked up at a television set tuned to CNN. An injured U.S. soldier was on the screen, being attended to by a medic. "They shouldn't show this on TV," the reporter said to the room full of our colleagues. Then, warming up to his theme, he continued, "This is what lost us the Vietnam War, showing the wounded. They shouldn't show this stuff!" When that reporter read reports from the war to his audience, they deserved to know his point of view. It had to taint his story choice, the words he used on the air, and even his vocal inflections. We cannot hide what we think and believe just because we are reporters, and we shouldn't try.

I wrote a book about soldiers returning from the Iraq War who were opposed to the war because of their experiences there (*Mission Rejected*). I made clear my own opposition to the Iraq War and briefly recounted my experiences opposing the Vietnam War back when I was subject to the military draft. My application for conscientious objector status was denied by my draft board, and I included that personal history in the Iraq book along with a quote from the Selective Service psychiatrist who gauged me and the army incompatible, suggesting I was "a markedly eccentric young man, completely incapable of fitting into or complying with any authority structure." That background gives my readers a clear cue about my point of view. My next job was to serve those readers with clarity, fairness, and accuracy. Like me, Fox News broadcasts with a political agenda and they don't hide it. Al Jazeera doesn't report critical news about the government of Qatar, which owns it.

Transparency, suggest some journalism pundits including City University of New York Graduate School of Journalism professor Jeff Jarvis, is the new objectivity. We journalists really do not have a choice but to embrace transparency. We rarely are information gatekeepers any longer, even of our own proclivities. News consumers can search our personal backgrounds and get specific results after just seconds of clicks on a keyboard. Search a little deeper and they can find alternative and primary sources for the stories we write. So much for any lip service to objectivity; our prejudices are on public display. Google my name and the words "Vietnam War" and the first hit will inform you that I was a war resister. Transparency is the new objectivity, indeed.

The Slow News rule is: Know your sources and their prejudices.

Rule 12: Seek information about news stories from multiple sources

When President Obama announced that U.S. forces had killed Osama bin Laden, I skipped the talking heads at CNN and Fox News, and instead studied the commentary offered by Al Jazeera's English-language channel. The next day I didn't just read about the details in *The New York Times* that's still delivered the old-fashioned style: a folded paper is thrown in my driveway at dawn by the deliverywoman. I read the London *Independent* for a view from Europe and I retrieved reports from the dominant Pakistani English-language newspaper, *Dawn*.

The last time I had used *Dawn* as a resource was in Karachi. I was researching the case of an American woman locked up in squalid Central Prison for smuggling heroin. It was 1985 and the entrance to *Dawn's* offices was off an alley next to a foul-smelling creek. I remember trying to keep my breathing shallow as I climbed the stairs that led to the newspaper's antiquated offices. I opened the door and it was like stepping into newspaper history. There were no computer workstations in the newsroom; I was working for NBC News at the time and our newsroom was already computer equipped. Heck, there weren't even electric typewriters at *Dawn*. There was no computer database in the library to help with a search of the newspaper's back issues, just huge scrapbooks filled with yellowed clippings from back issues. Under a slight breeze from slow-turning overhead fans, I studied the narcotics stories file, breathing the pungent aroma of newspaper and ink, a nice antidote to the stink that wafted up from the creek. Today I can search *Dawn's* back issues and read today's news sitting in my office at the University of Oregon, over seventy-five hundred miles from the newspaper's Pakistan newsroom.

The Slow News rule is to avoid single sources. Of course we must read our hometown newspapers. It makes sense to keep track of what so-called newspapers of record like *The New York Times* report. But it should be second nature for us to go to multiple sources when we're interested in a complex and controversial story, especially since we can make that connection from the comfort of our living rooms.

The techniques are easy and obvious. If a story is controversial, look for news reports from outlets that seek to avoid bias, like the BBC, but also find news sources that favor or are influenced by specific points of view. For example, after the U.S. government reported that it had killed Osama bin Laden, few news reports questioned the claim, even though there was no body and the alleged photographic evidence of bin Laden's death was kept from the public (not that photographs would be universally believed in this era of Photoshop). I'm not suggesting that bin Laden is still alive and that the U.S. government conspired to fake his death. But it is worthwhile to consider reports that differ from the official line.

The former *New York Times* foreign correspondent Chris Hedges, for example, spoke at a fundraiser for the Internet-based news organization Truthdig the evening bin Laden's death was announced. Hedges, the author of several books and a Truthdig columnist, was in New York City on September 11, 2001, and he shared a Pulitzer Prize for his work covering al Qaida. He chose his words carefully that evening saying "reportedly Osama bin Laden was killed" and "if it is correct that Osama bin Laden is dead." Reflecting on the actions of the U.S. government in response to the 9/11 attacks he said, "I despair that we as a country, as Nietzsche understood, have become the monster we are attempting to fight."

Hedges' point of view was radically different from the cover of the special edition of the *New York Post* the next day, which screamed, "GOT HIM! Vengeance at last! U.S. nails the bastard." Its tabloid rival, the *Daily News*, offered a forward look for the story with its splash, "ROT IN HELL." Reading them both, and plenty of what comes in between Hedges and the tabloids (the *Asian Age* headlined from Delhi, "U.S. KILLS BIN LADEN IN (YOU KNEW IT) PAKISTAN"), helps us figure out and develop our own feelings and beliefs.

Reliable sources are a click away on the Internet, but misinformation (and its worse cousin, disinformation) can spread with the click of a keyboard as well. Using magical Internet tools requires that careful attention be paid to sources. Consider the millions of Facebook and

Twitter users who read and then spread their thoughts about bin Laden's death via a quote they thought was taken from a speech by Dr. Martin Luther King, Jr.: "I will mourn the loss of thousands of precious lives, but I will not rejoice in the death of one, not even an enemy." A blogger at *The Atlantic* did the necessary homework and determined that the poetic response to the bin Laden killing came from Jessica Dovey, who had recently graduated from Penn State. She followed her own thought with a line from King's book, *Strength to Love*: "Returning hate for hate multiplies hate, adding deeper darkness to a night already devoid of stars. Darkness cannot drive out darkness; only light can do that. Hate cannot drive out hate, only love can do that," and started sending it around to her friends. They, as is so common, started sending the poignant lines to their friends, and in the process dropped the quote marks that separated Ms. Dovey's language from Dr. King's. In later iterations, King's words were dropped and Ms. Dovey's line was attributed to him.

The Slow News rule regarding multiple sources mandates that those sources be vetted carefully. Hoaxes and mistakes, along with the mindless ramblings of countless bloggers, pack the Internet. Don't allow yourself to be trapped into believing and repeating reports that you don't check. Transparency may be the new objectivity. But verifying and attributing continue to be the critical paths to finding credible news. As my former boss at NBC News, Jim Farley, used to explain, "If your mother says she loves you, check it."

Rule 13: Find primary sources

The depth and agility of computer-assisted reporting is not limited to the professional reporter. Make yourself an adjunct journalist and provide corroborating evidence and background to the news you consume.

Only a few years ago many of the tools of the journalism profession (or is it a craft or a trade?) were difficult or impossible for a layman to access. Journalists—good journalists—worked hard developing sources to provide them with access to privileged information; they still do. But the combination of the Internet and the freedom of information laws that exist in a growing number of countries make it possible for citizens to sit at home in front of a computer screen trolling for primary sources to cross-check what's in the daily paper or spewing out of the TV.

The tried-and-true saying, "Don't believe everything you read in the newspaper," works even better for the often unfiltered chatter that fills the Internet. User-generated content has its value (who doesn't want to reconnect with old school chums?), but an anonymous tweet can't compete as news with a primary source. There are "official" Twitter accounts; Twitter itself identifies them so users can be sure that the 140 characters really are coming from the White House or Lady Gaga (as long as the system hasn't been hacked). But the Twittersphere is jammed with unknown "followers" and "followed" and the babble of re-tweeters repeating and restating their version of "news" only exacerbates the media-generated waste of time.

Here's a bizarre example from Texas. The story starts in Liberty County when a woman called police, eventually directing them to a home where blood was smeared on the front porch and the stink of rotting flesh was in the air. Police checked out the scene, of course, especially since the woman—who identified herself as a prophetess ("I get my information from Jesus and the angels")—worried to investigators that she was experiencing visions of children in jeopardy. While the cops searched the property, the world of Twitter came alive.

"Thirty bodies of children found just 51 miles northeast of Houston in Hardin," tweeted @the_feral_child. The anonymity of such a Twitter message mocks the idea that it is a valid news report. But that didn't dampen the strange concern of @MsLivia who commented to all bothering to listen, "Hopefully a lot of loved ones find their missing family." Why would MsLivia hope someone missing a child would find the body? Wouldn't it be more appropriate that she hope the child be found alive and well? But, again, the more basic reality: This is not news. This is gossip masquerading as news. @HannahTheBloody adds to the confusion with a heartfelt, "Prayers and thoughts to the people of Hardin and the lives that have been lost." @AtoBoldon checked in with, "Law enforcement sources tell CBS News a mass grave with dismembered bodies has been found in Harden." At this point no bodies—dismembered or otherwise—had been found, nor had police told any CBS reporters otherwise.

The facts on the ground did not keep @Unique1384 from reporting to anyone who bothered to listen, "Cops found at least 30 dismembered bodies buried in Hardin." @MelissaSWEETS added the tantalizing detail, ". . . mostly children," and @kplosee offered the commentary, "This is about to be a HUGE story!" A hint of skepticism was injected by @WSTJBob who asked, "Rhetorical question: How hard or easy is it to get national attention on a plot of land in Harden, TX?" @carmelmelouney added to the fray with a tweet that at least offers attribution, "AP [Associated Press] reports Liberty County Judge Craig McNair said an anonymous tipster claiming to be a psychic said multiple bodies buried in Hardin, TX." And @redsox1974 checked in with a note impossible to refute, "I have no idea what is going on in Hardin."

At this point, one of my students at the University of Oregon School of Journalism and Communication, Kylie Keppler, whom I thank for bringing this example to my attention, no longer could restrain herself. She found it (understandably) necessary to check in and set the record straight. "They are INVESTIGATING a TIP of a POSSIBLE mass grave," she wrote under her nom de plume @MarieSleeps. "No corpses have been found at this time." She added her source: CBS News. That didn't stem the imagination of @LadyyTina who exclaimed, "Wow, does anybody else see this Hardin mass grave story??" She was followed by @romulasry who offered, using journalese style, "BREAKING: 30 bodies found at home in TEXAS including those of children." One after another the false reports continued to bounce around the Twittersphere, begging the question: Why, even were the story true, would the gossipers bother to swap these stories? If, in fact, a crime had been committed, there was no need to speculate. There was no need to rush to try to figure out what occurred. Credibly sourced reports from journalists on the scene would have satisfied morbid curiosity as soon as the cops finished their search.

Waiting for yesterday's news until tomorrow would have served these curious Twitter addicts just fine. The fact that half of these hasty users claim to work in the news media business shows how easy it is to forget common sense when communicating via a medium such as Twitter.

A tweet from @DevorahLeah's was spat out as a post mortem to the flurry of cyber-concern reads, "Reporters & police suckered by a psychic." But the reporters and police were not suckered. They did their jobs. Rex Evans, the Liberty County Sheriff's spokesman, summed up the professional side of the affair with the succinct, "I just wish that people would understand that, as a law enforcement agency, we're obligated to investigate things, and yesterday was simply us conducting an investigation to find out factual information. There was nothing more." The only something more was Twitter gossip. Or as @dtollison wrote, wasting still more pixels, "Mass grave in Hardin turned out to be false—thank goodness! Happy to be wrong in my last tweet."

The Hardin non-story reminds me of the old party game called telephone. The players gather in a circle, remember? The game starts when one player whispers into the ear of another some statement of fact or fancy. The message is passed around the circle and—invariably—when it finally returns to the first sender it barely resembles the original.

What about the blood on the porch and the stink from the house? Police investigators determined that the blood was weeks old, left over from an attempted suicide by an absent-without-leave soldier, and the stinky smell really was rotting flesh: inside a broken freezer was decomposing pork crawling with maggots.

The silliness of the Texas stampede does not negate the value of crowd sourcing, nor does it negate the value of Twitter and Facebook and other social media as tools for people to stay in touch or organize—whether a party or a revolution. Journalists have always relied on the potential value of news tips. But news tips are just that, tips. Not primary sources. Twitter of course can host primary sources, including credible journalists. But, as Garry Trudeau lampooned in *Doonesbury* with its comic strip Twitter-addict TV reporter Roland Hedley, just because a tweet comes from an account holder who is a reporter doesn't necessarily mean that the blurb transmitted is worth reading. An example? "Been working on my blog," Hedley tweets. "Just posted an item reporting I was about to tweet. Really good comments so far."

The Slow News rule: Expecting so-called "citizen journalists" to replace news reporting based on investigations using primary sources and eyewitness accounts of events is a fool's errand. "Citizen journalism," contends journalist Andrew Stroehlein from his desk at the International Crisis Group in Brussels, where he studies conflict, "is like citizen dentistry." His is a painful image, and it's an important reminder of the often-dangerous skilled legwork professional journalists perform for society. Without their work we're at the mercy of amateur gossipers and professional manipulators. "You get away with things like Iraq," Stroehlein says about the lies the second President Bush told to rationalize his war there, "because people don't know what's going on."

Rule 14: Look for news close to home

Chats over the back fence and in the barbershop or café often provide more informed sources about news of consequence to your day-to-day life than the pontificating, self-serving talking heads on television "news" programs. Local newspapers build communities and keep neighbors informed about news that big media understandably ignores.

When I lived on the Sonoma County coast in California, *Business Week* named Bodega Bay, my home then, one of the most expensive small towns in America. Bodega Bay is world famous as the locale where Alfred Hitchcock shot his film *The Birds*. From the deck of my house you could see the place where the actress Tippi Hedren was first attacked by a seagull. Shortly after *Business Week* anointed Bodega Bay with luxury status the *Santa Rosa Press Democrat* newspaper responded to the news with the headline, "Worth the price."

Plenty of car bumpers in Bodega Bay sport the too-cute sticker that reads, "Bodega Bay—a quaint little drinking village with a fishing problem." In fact, one of the most serious problems with Bodega Bay was neither fishing nor drinking. It was that this jewel on the Pacific coast—the place I called home—lacked even a remote sense of community.

Part of the problem was geographic. Bodega Bay stretches for a few miles hugging the coastline, and its few streets are just offshoots of its main drag: Highway One, the coast road that stretches from Mexico north through California toward the Oregon border. In the summertime and on weekends Highway One is jammed with tourist traffic, and the lack of sidewalks and shoulders makes walking treacherous. There is no focal point in Bodega Bay, no crossroads. Bodega Bay offers no main square, no village green, no natural and traditional gathering point.

Since the remodeling of the Tides restaurant (the place where a bloody Tippi Hedren sought help in the movie), there's no saloon featuring the type of atmosphere that attracts tourists and locals alike. The modernized Tides looks and feels more like an airport departure lounge than a place to play liars dice and tell fish stories. There is no library, no bookstore, no hardware store, no drug store soda fountain, and no city park in Bodega Bay.

The closest thing to a community center is the post office. If I happened to show up at the same time to collect my mail as a neighbor, we would exchange a quick hello and perhaps an update about people and places we held in common. Funeral notices were posted ad hoc on the post office doors, and if we were lucky when we checked our mailboxes, clerks Jaime, Sue, or Mary might offer a taste of local gossip to spice up the visit.

Exacerbating the geographic and commercial challenges to community building was the social and economic stratification of the place. At the south end of town is Bodega Harbour, or "Harbor with a 'U'" as my wife calls it in an effort to mock the pretentiousness it exhibits by adopting the British spelling of the word. Bodega Harbour is a golf course surrounded by fancy houses, most of them vacation rentals. On the west side of the bay, the University of California Marine Laboratory draws more short timers: students and researchers. Old Town maintains the last vestiges of the fishermen and their wives who built the first houses along the bay. Abalone shells decorate their yards and boats sit on trailers alongside motor homes. Old Town still feels blue-collar. The house trailers and cabins at Porto Bodega house much of the town's Mexican immigrant community.

But despite all of these challenges to community, a viable weekly Bodega Bay newspaper would serve a vital purpose: it would bring the thousand or so individualists who live there together on its pages. It would introduce them to each other and tell what's happening in their midst. It would unite this disparate collection of strangers who for whatever reason chose to settle there and it would help explain them to each other.

In the late 1990s the *Bodega Bay Navigator* newspaper sputtered and finally put its last issue to bed. It stopped printing and moved its operation to a minimal Internet presence. "Not enough advertising dollars," explained editor and publisher Joel Hack (great name for a newspaperman, Hack). "Bodega Bay is a small retail market, and the merchants in Sebastopol and Santa Rosa don't need us." Hack's slap-dash Navigator Internet site is no replacement for a running commentary on local life produced with ink on paper (what an editor I worked with at the *San Francisco Chronicle* called "the dead tree edition"). A hard copy weekly newspaper sits on the kitchen table for days and is read and reread. Stories from it are torn out and stuck on refrigerators or sent to distant friends and relatives. Back issues are stored in libraries.

We can't know what's going on in our midst if no one is lurking around, asking questions, and compiling reports. There is no dearth of news in Bodega Bay, news that is important to local residents but not worth the bother for the *Press Democrat* headquartered almost an hour east in the county seat, Santa Rosa, a newspaper with no beat reporter assigned to the Sonoma County coast. The town suffers from two unsolved murders. Without a newspaper, who is providing oversight of the sheriff's investigations? The fishing economy is in crisis; what is being done to restore the fishery? Construction started on a long-delayed and controversial housing project; who is watching to make sure the developer adheres to the terms of his permit? What's going on at the Coast Guard station? Who's watching the results of our Fire Board and Utility District meetings? What goes on in the windowless Grange Hall? Who is preaching what up at the Union Church? Where is the record of births and deaths, marriages, and high school graduations?

A town without a newspaper is a town at risk. A community newspaper, lamented Hack when he talked to me about closing the *Navigator*, "teaches a community how to talk to itself." He cites the California car culture, the hours we spend in front of the television, and our tendency to exist in personal cocoons as examples of our growing isolation and alienation. "There are a gazillion things that work against community," he says, "and a newspaper is one of the things that offsets lack of community."

A town's character is influenced by its physical location and its architecture. But its mythology and sense of self develops as events occur. And we can't all be everywhere talking with everyone about what's going on around town. Bodega Bay needs a witness to chronicle those events, to put them into historical perspective. Newspaper reporters and editors perform those critical community-building roles. Bodega Bay needs a curmudgeonly editor-in-chief poking around and commenting on other people's business, someone who loves Bodega Bay and prints stories that help us question and understand ourselves.

Back in the mid-1970s I was the founding editor of the *Gold Hill News*, a newspaper serving the steady new immigration from urban California that was starting to repopulate the Comstock, a region in Nevada mined for its rich silver and gold ore since the Civil War days. Actually, I was not really the founding editor, but rather editor of the resuscitated newspaper. The *News* was established back in editor Alf Doten's time, when Mark Twain was writing at the competing *Territorial Enterprise*, and it first closed down in the early 1880s, as the gold and silver boom days turned to bust. We brought it back to life ninety-two years later with a front-page announcement apologizing to readers for any inconvenience the hiatus had caused. The resurgent *News* enjoyed a well-received reincarnation, just one more example of the human need to be connected. Bringing us together is a role played by newspapers throughout much of Nevada's history.

Small-town newspapers in Nevada and elsewhere struggle. Most classified advertising is a memory, replaced by instantaneous and free Internet-based advertising services like Craigslist. Display advertising, those full-page ads for department and grocery stores, are placed with less frequency as businesses work to increase their profit margins. Tight money makes subscribers think twice about home delivery of the newspaper. What once was a routine purchase is vulnerable to family budget cuts, especially when much of its contents is available free via the Internet.

As revenues decrease, owners of newspapers small and large understandably are resistant to spending money on the industry's core competence: reporting the news. Layoffs and buyouts of reporters and editors decimate newsrooms. The trickle-down effect is devastating to the watchdog role journalism plays in society, and not only because newspapers are thin remnants of their recent selves. Trace most news you receive over the radio, from TV, or through your favorite Internet portal, and you'll see that the original gumshoe work usually was a newspaper reporter's. Yes, an increasing number of stories are being developed on independent websites devoted to news, and by bloggers creatively trolling cyberspace from their equivalent of Left Bank garrets. The medium may be at least part of the message, but when news is the goal the platform is subservient to content. Expecting noise on the Internet to replace professional newsgathering individuals and organizations is like trying to look at your Facebook stuff on a Mac Classic with a dial-up connection. Maybe that's a metaphor that's too mixed, but the intent is clear: it won't work.

The original *Gold Hill News* blamed its death in 1882 on "the great depression in business interests of this town . . . and unfavorable prospects for the near future." That's a headline that—sad to report—could be today's. The newspaper business must reinvent itself quickly to avoid once again printing its own obituaries.

The Slow News rule: Support your local community newspaper, and renew your subscription.

Rule 15: Avoid provincialism

When he was running CNN, the network he founded, Ted Turner famously forbade his news correspondents from using the word "foreign" to describe a country not the United States: Replace "foreign" with "overseas" or "international," he told his troops. Despite the fact that CNN was headquartered in Atlanta, he sought to create a borderless news brand. And he succeeded. We can accomplish the same goal with our own personal news consumption and avoid the plagues of provincialism. The Slow News rule is: We are all cosmopolitans with an easy few keystrokes.

Contrast and compare news stories in your newspaper with the reportage of the same events covered by papers with alternative priorities and loyalties. English is our contemporary lingua franca, and just about every place in the world offers a look at the news through their local eyes via the English language.

A typical example is the coverage of the 2011 earthquake, tsunami, and nuclear power plant disaster in Japan. A trip around the newspaper world offered varied points of view and a much wider range of information about the crises than we would experience were we to just stick with hometown news outlets. Of course at least some due diligence is required regarding the prejudices of newspapers we encounter on such Internet searches; that requirement is covered in Rule 11.

From the *Budapest Times* ("Understanding Hungary" is their motto) the worry was the effect of problems in Japan on Japanese manufacturing companies making products in Hungary (where wages are relatively low by European standards). Suzuki Hungary spokeswoman Viktória Ruska, for example, told the paper that some six weeks worth of Japanese-made parts are stockpiled in Hungary so there was no immediate worry about production.

The Times of India internationalized the earthquake story with a report from Gurgaon about Indian families concerned about their relatives working in Japan.

The Sydney Morning Herald followed up on the 'quake with a story headlined, "Let's keep the Japanese earthquake in perspective," by one Patrick McKenzie, a business owner living in Japan, who complained, "Some of the English-language reporting on the Japanese disaster has been so bad that my mother is worried for my safety." He acted perplexed by those with a poor command of Japanese geography who feared extensive damage in Tokyo, where, when he wrote his report, one death was blamed on the temblor. "By comparison, on any given Friday, Tokyo will typically have more deaths caused by traffic accidents."

From Toronto's *Globe and Mail* came an attempt to keep Japan's catastrophe from panicking Canadians. Don't allow worry about radiation in the seawater to keep you from eating sushi, the paper advised, quoting a scientist who tried to put the contamination in perspective, from his sardonic point of view. "You have to eat a million kilograms of seaweed to get the dose which is equivalent to the dose of a cancer treatment," said Simon Fraser University chemist Krzysztof Starosta. "And it has to be dried. You will die of dehydration rather than radiation poisoning."

The Communist Party mouthpiece *China Daily* used the news to express its neighborly concern, reporting that Chinese Premier Wen Jiabao planned a trip to the disaster zone. The paper said he told a group of Japanese business leaders visiting Beijing, "I will visit disaster-hit areas to express my sympathy to the Japanese people, convey the friendly sentiment of the Chinese people and their sincere support for the country's reconstruction efforts."

The Italian news agency Adnkronos offered an English-language international version. On March 15, four days after the explosion at the Fukushima power plant, it reported an announcement by Enel, Italy's largest electricity producer (the Italian government is its largest shareholder): despite the fears of a nuclear disaster, the plan to bring back nuclear energy production in Italy after twenty-four years would go on unchanged. "Italy is a highly seismic zone. A 2008 earthquake struck the central city of L'Aquila, killing about three hundred people," Adnkronos noted in its news story. Impossible to miss the irony as Enel attempted to bolster public support by claiming its plants were failsafe even after the

Japan accident. A referendum held the following June showed the public was not convinced and a moratorium was imposed on nuclear energy production in Italy.

The coverage of the Japan disaster varied country by country depending on national priorities. When an issue involves players from different countries, direct access to their various views helps us grasp the essence of the story through their eyes. Consider the controversy surrounding the extradition of the Italian convicted criminal Cesare Battisti. Over several years, twenty-four Italian justices judged him guilty of various crimes, including multiple murders. In 1979 he was sentenced to prison, but he escaped first to France and then to Brazil, which refused to send him back to Italy and granted him political refugee status. Many officials and commentators in France and Brazil opposed the Italian courts' rulings, and by reading dispatches from all three countries news consumers throughout the world can access the contradictory opinions. Listening to these differing pronouncements about Battisti's status (even if they are wrong) is crucial for an understanding of how the story has evolved. The Italians may learn why some people in France were so stubborn about rejecting Italy's request that he be extradited (they were invoking the Mitterrand doctrine, a policy that offered asylum to convicted criminals wanted for violent political acts) and why influential Brazilian politicians also consider Battisti a political refugee. The French and the Brazilians, at the same time, may better comprehend Italy's stance regarding Battisti by paying attention to Italian news sources. All those facts and opinions are just a click away.

When news breaks, it takes just minutes to circumnavigate the globe from the comfort of our living rooms, a worthwhile practice that contributes to Rule 11's goal of keeping propaganda and bias in perspective.

The Slow News rule is: Jump past national frontiers (easy to do with the Internet) and consume "foreign" sources. Appreciate the different approaches that different nationalities and cultures take to specific stories and news reporting.

Rule 16: Buy some of your news

In a world of easy-to-obtain free information (polluted by endless misinformation and disinformation), there are times when it is worth investing time and/or money for worthwhile news content. News consumers are easy targets for news that is offered for free. The argument for buying news has a distinct corollary: when news is free, ask why. Who expects to benefit from its free distribution and what is the (hidden?) agenda?

Of course selling advertisements adjacent to the news product is a time-tested device for making money from the news (and for paying for news reporting). But some corporate owners of newsgathering organizations lose sight of (or just fail to care about) the quality of the news they purvey. When answering to shareholders trumps a sense of public service, it's easy to rationalize the search for methods to save money and still generate content that appears to be news. Talk radio is a fine example: radio announcers yelling at listeners about the news hardly counts as news. Celebrity "news" is another empty-calories technique for filling up pages or air time. The publicity machine for movie stars and politicians (sometimes the same person, eh, Arnold Schwarzenegger?) cranks out endless material about their clients for print and broadcast. Why hire a reporter when you can just repackage the free stuff?

Reporting takes time and costs money. Trained and experienced journalists can't do their work for free. We pay for the gas and the electricity in our homes; gas stations charge us to pour fuel in our car tanks. It's frowned upon to eat in a restaurant and not pay the bill. If we think of news as another commodity—something we need in our daily lives—then it makes sense to expect to pay for it. There is journalism of value available without a direct cash cost to the consumer. Advertising-supported newspapers like those of the Metro group or the *Village Voice* are distributed free. An abundance of newspapers still offer their reporting on websites without the barrier of a paywall and stories that require a fee to read are reposted on easy-to-find free sites. No money is needed to use commercial-saturated television and radio. It's an indirect charge: you must deal with the interruption from the advertising while you wonder if the advertising influences the news coverage. But whatever the revenue model, you usually get what you pay for. And if there is no cost for your news, you might consider that it's worth what you paid for it.

In the UK it is illegal to use a TV and tune it to BBC television if you do not pay your license fees. If you want to watch the news in color, it will cost you a couple of hundred bucks a year. You can save a bundle if you can find a black and white TV. That throwback to the 1950s commands less than a hundred dollars for a license. In Italy the license fee is about a hundred and fifty dollars. Oddly enough, as is the case in many countries where such a charge is imposed, it must be paid by anyone who possesses a device able to receive the TV signal: it is a tax on the possession of the devices themselves, regardless of their use.

As newspapers struggle to figure out how to charge for their online content, more and more are hiding some of their good stuff behind a paywall. Rather than trying to circumvent their efforts via an easy workaround, consider how inexpensive it is to pay the bill and hope the money is used for good journalism. At the *Financial Times* an online subscription is about the price of a caffe latte, and that's for a week of news; it's about the same for *The New York Times*; a little cheaper for *The Wall Street Journal*. Buy your newspaper and support its advertisers so that it can support the journalists.

The Slow News rule: Since you get what you pay for, consider buying some news.

Rule 17: Evade news-like assaults that merely convey commercials

We are barraged by news and pseudo-news. The cacophony assaults us in some of the most unexpected places, almost always with advertisements adjacent to the information. The walls above urinals in men's rest rooms are no longer the exclusive domain of graffiti writers. It is not uncommon to be faced with a newspaper pinned to the wall, and some facilities now are equipped with video monitors spewing advertising and other information. Jump in a taxicab in New York City and as soon as the cabbie drops the flag on the meter, the video monitor clicks on. We must proactively opt out—figure out how to turn off the sound and picture— otherwise we're subjected to a local TV announcer regurgitating the day's news, interspersed with ads. Stop at a gas station and don't be surprised if a video monitor is mounted above the gas pump. These do not even offer the opportunity of an on-off switch. They scream out the news blurbs and commercials as we buy fuel. Waiting for a flight in an airport departure lounge? CNN is likely waiting there with you, again with no off switch. Supermarket check-out lines often include the ubiquitous video screen, and as we, a captive audience, wait to pay for our groceries, the tube tries to convince us to buy more stuff, ads mixed with food "news" we didn't request. In the spring of 2013 I took a colleague out to lunch at the Old Ebbitt Grill in Washington, one of the DC haunts where it is as much fun to watch the hustling patrons as to eat the crab cakes. Attached to the bill was another slip printed when the waiter ran my credit card, a page titled "The Latest News" and filled with Associated Press headlines. There is a BBC announcer blabbing news headlines on the express train from Heathrow to Paddington Station (unless you choose to take the "quiet car" which is TV free and where mobile phone use is forbidden). There are screens broadcasting an unbalanced mixture of ads and news (more ads than news, of course) along the tracks in Milan subway stations. Those that are mounted along Trenitalia's tracks don't even make an attempt at broadcasting interesting news; they just blast a repetition of

70

advertisements that pour down on the audience of travelers with nowhere to hide from the media assault while waiting for their trains. The elevators in a Chicago office building where I hold periodic meetings are equipped with video screens barking news briefs and ads between floors. Even driving down the highway in the privacy of your own car it's sometimes impossible to escape TV. Screens mounted for backseat viewers are distractingly visible to drivers in other cars.

Since these pseudo-newscasts are just filler or, worse, ads dressed up with some news flavor, we consumers need to be awake to their charms and actively resist them. Remember to bring a book with you when you travel or bring your own music in your iPod or relatively smart phone. If you're really hungry for news, there's always some newsstand somewhere close to you where you can buy real news or real entertainment—stuff you choose for yourself instead of allowing yourself to be a captive audience for brain clutter.

The Slow News rule: Don't allow yourself to be subjected to news just because it is everywhere. Choose for yourself what news sources you will consume, and when. Look away from the imposing video flicker—and daydream.

Rule 18: Avoid "news reports" pretending to be something they are not

One of the most onerous and devious methods developed by the public relations industry to intrude on journalism is the press release masquerading as legitimate news. As TV outlets seek to cut expenses, PR specialists jump to fill the gap. They produce complete news-like packages, often with actors portraying news reporters interviewing "newsmakers." These "newsmakers" are, in reality, the PR firms' clients, and the "news report" is crafted to do nothing but promote the clients' products, services, or points of view. The TV news shows that make use of these video news releases (VNRs) should make it clear to their audiences that the package was not produced in an independent newsroom but rather came from a self-interested third party. Such disclaimers do not always accompany the slickly produced VNRs, and when faux news reporters are used they often end with a nondescript formal close at the completion of the story that makes it all but impossible to know the provenance of the "news report." Even if there is a caveat announced before the report begins, if the insert is well written and edited, and if it exhibits compelling videography, the viewer could well dismiss the disclaimer and interpret the PR message as news. That's the idea.

An example is the campaign from the French company Piper-Heidsieck to draw attention to their new champagne bottle, created by fashion designer Jean Paul Gaultier. The slick videos offered to TV and web TV outlets feature fast-cuts of the glitterati at the Cannes film festival, a quote from the Piper-Heidsieck CEO Anne-Charlotte Amory, which features her romantically French-accented English, and Gaultier himself, who explains that the champagne bottle "is covered by fishnet stocking, so that's quite sexy." Various versions of the videos may be found, of differing lengths and with or without soundtrack, presumably to make their use easier according to the needs of the outlets that will use them.

VNRs may be mistaken for news on the website of the Italian newspaper *la Repubblica*. In one example case, beside the video window, the written commentary headline sounds like a news report: "Boring trips are over: car windows become tablets." But it is plainly a Toyota commercial, and it's in English; not even the language has been adapted to accommodate the Italian audience—or perhaps the client believes the English adds prestige to its message.

Businesses, professional organizations, and governments all make use of VNRs. The U.S. military operates what it calls the Defense Video and Imagery Distribution System. From the DVIDS website, TV outlets can download video packages such as "a monthly half-hour program showcasing the latest action from the field" titled *In the Fight*. In one episode, guns blaze, jets scream, and tanks blast, as the soft, female voice-over artist announces, "It was a day that will go down as a major historical event in U.S. history," before she introduces U.S. soldiers reacting to the death of Osama bin Laden. The video comes complete with a music bed, which may make it difficult for a local TV station to rationalize using it as if it were an independent news report. But in the YouTube era, Video News Release producers easily bypass traditional media and find new audiences via the Internet.

The public relations industry is ready to help get VNRs out to waiting eyeballs. PR Newswire, for example, will distribute VNRs via its pervasive website for a fee, and production companies worldwide are equipped to create them, rife with product placement.

Karen Ryan is a public relations practitioner who once was employed by American television news departments. She decided the video news release business was more to her liking and she achieved some notoriety when propaganda pieces she created for the U.S. government were exposed as violating government policies because they were designed to appear as if they were independent news reports. After the scandal broke, Ryan told *The New York Times* that she was surprised how many local TV stations aired her packages without editing them or identifying their origin to viewers. The *Times* reporter asked her if she would have aired her VNRs when she worked in broadcast news as a reporter.

"Absolutely not" was her answer.

The Slow News rule: Know your suppliers, be they food, drink, or information.

Rule 19: Consider journalists as a noise filter

News is only the first draft of history. Despite the expectation of credibility that comes with words on paper or a screen and with sonorous voices of doom on the radio or TV, check the news you're fed. The first draft of history often is inaccurate. Especially in this age of instant news via Twitter and Facebook, it's not just the gossips among us who spread unsubstantiated stories; the news professionals themselves find it difficult to resist the impulse to punch "send" with only fragments of a story in their notebooks.

Sometimes the lies come out of the newsroom, and the editors are as blindsided as their customers. Jayson Blair was a star *New York Times* reporter before he was exposed as a plagiarizer and a liar. He stole other reporters' copy and he fictionalized his own. When I spoke with him for a story I was working on about ethics, he called his case an important lesson for journalism (and a personal tragedy). He was motivated to lie, he told me, out of an "eagerness to please and because of pressure to live up to expectations. I took on way too much. I never said no. I always wanted people to believe that I could accomplish insurmountable things. I think that catches a lot of people and it's a lot easier for them to lie their way around something or fake something than it is to just be honest and say, 'I can't do it.'"

Blair's career soared, fueled by his dramatic fraudulent stories, but he was miserable. "I didn't intend to deceive anyone. I wasn't getting a kick out of it." He knows he left a terrible journalistic legacy. "There are certain lies that if you take a look at the stories that I wrote they were lies that hurt editors. There were lies that hurt other reporters who flew on the reputation of the *Times*. There were lies that hurt me. There were lies that hurt the subject of the stories to varying degrees. For some of the people who were written about it didn't bother them at all but it bothered the journalistic community tremendously. Other ones didn't really bother journalists at all but really actually caused harm for the people who were being written about."

But back to noise and journalists. Of course there are millions addicted to tweeting and reading the tweets of others. *New York Times* media critic David Carr is one of the users. He lusts after the interruption tweets inject into his routine and rhapsodized about it in his column. "There is always something more interesting on Twitter than whatever you happen to be working on."

Nonsense, responded *The New Yorker* magazine writer George Packer, despite his lack of experience with Twitter. "Who doesn't want to be taken out of the boredom or pain of the present at any given moment?" he asked his readers. "That's what drugs are for, and that's why people become addicted to them. Twitter," he insisted, "is crack for media addicts." Predictably Packer was criticized not just for his anti-Twitter stance but for criticizing it without trying the service. He responded by pointing out that he hasn't tried crack, either. The exchange reminds me of my interview with a state senator who drafted the law prohibiting cockfighting in Louisiana. He told me that when opponents of his bill asked him how he could be against what they consider a sport when he had never witnessed a cockfight, he asked them if they had ever witnessed an abortion.

But seeking and desiring incoming new information can be an addiction. I know I tend to punch up my email even before my morning cup of green tea is brewed. Worse, I know I experience a psychological letdown if my inbox is empty. It's not just my ego ("Nobody wrote to me, nobody must care!"), it's that the rush of adrenaline is missing. No news may be good news. But no news means nothing is new. If nothing is new we're forced to deal with the existing residue, and that can be tough and dirty work. The time and effort required to keep up with the day's news—both public and private—can help us rationalize procrastinating about other duties we face.

I know the search for the latest breaking news is one of the lures of journalism for me. Every day for a reporter, under the best of circumstances, is an adventure into the unknown and an opportunity to learn first what no one else yet knows. I've enjoyed the excitement of scooping the competition, being first with the story even if only by seconds. Here's a silly example: when I was reporting on the trial of newspaper heiress

Patty Hearst for the NBC News radio division (in those ancient days before ubiquitous mobile telephones), I plotted with a confederate who commandeered a public telephone in the courthouse lobby so that I could race out of the courtroom and announce the verdict to America moments before my compatriots from the ABC and CBS radio news departments. Did it matter to the audience? Of course not. But it was an amusing (and adrenaline pumping) exercise.

News reporting requires a filter. Incoming information needs to be curated. Factoids and propaganda and other bits and pieces of a news story need to be fact checked and vetted. Claims and counterclaims must be investigated. An independent observer should note events, if we hope for some balance when we hear about what occurred. If we jettison the journalist, much of the information being generated is just noise without context. I'm not contradicting the idea that we all can be journalists. I'm reinforcing the need for journalists.

Consider the journalistic role of a book reviewer for example, or a restaurant reviewer. When self-selected anonymous reviewers show up on Amazon and claim a book is not worth reading, why should we pay attention to these opinions? We do not know if the reviews were drafted by an enemy of the author of the book being trashed. Why should we waste time reading a review by a writer unknown to us, and unaffiliated with any organization that would hold the reviewer accountable? The same with amateur restaurant reviews, and all the other anonymous chatter that fills Internet comment pages.

Information out of context that's consumed as news can be devastating. Take the case of Shirley Sherrod for an example. A black woman, she worked for the Obama Administration in the USDA. In March 2010, a blogger posted an excerpt of a speech she delivered to the NAACP. During the speech she told the audience that she dedicated her life to civil rights work after her father was killed in a racist attack. She spoke of her efforts to help black farmers and recounted a request from a white couple for help with their farm. A clip of the speech that was excerpted out of context made it seem as if she did not want to help the whites. Had the clip been played in context it would have been clear that the reverse was true.

The clip in question was isolated by a blogger and picked up by Fox News and other media outlets. No effort was made to report the rest of the story, an example of journalism being practiced irresponsibly. The USDA fired Sherrod, and she was humiliated in the court of instant and incomplete public opinion. Days later the full video of her speech was released, making it clear that she did not discriminate against the white farmers; the white farmers in question came forward to commend her efforts on their behalf. The White House apologized. President Obama offered her a better job. Even the Fox News pundit Bill O'Reilly acknowledged that he owed Shirley Sherrod an apology.

The damage was done. She refused to rejoin the government. The USDA lost a valuable advocate.

The Slow News rule is: Noise is not news.

A corollary of this Slow News rule must be: Even if you're exposed to the voice and picture of a primary source, check on the context.

Part Three

**The Onus Is on
the News Consumer**

Rule 20: Think through the unintended consequences of making yourself news

While I was researching this book, a story was unfolding in Washington and New York that fuels my Slow News Movement. The former New York Congressman Anthony Weiner (who later ran for mayor of New York City) worked desperately to distance himself from a photograph showing the image of a sexually aroused man from the waist down wearing underwear, a picture in which nothing was left to a viewer's imagination. The snapshot became an issue for the congressman because records leaked to reporters indicated it was sent from Weiner's Twitter account to a twenty-one-year-old Whatcom Community College student far across the North American continent in Washington State. For over a week the congressman lashed out at his political enemies, claiming his Twitter account had been hacked and that he did not send the picture. However, in interview after interview, Weiner refused to state without equivocation that the photograph did not depict him. "Battle of the Bulge," read the headline in the *New York Post.* "This was essentially a hacked account that had a gag photo sent out on it," he insisted repeatedly, but then added, "I can't say with certainty very much about where the photograph came from." His vague quasi-denial regarding the provenance of the picture and whose body part it depicted only added to reporters' and the public's curiosity and skepticism.

Weiner was no subscriber to the Slow News Movement (although he may be one now). On the contrary, he embraced social media, keeping in touch with his constituents via an active Facebook account, and he was famous for a steady stream of tweets to the thousands and thousands of Twitter users "following him," to use the Twitter jargon. He spewed endlessly, from minutiae to international politics to—as it turned out—pornography. And then, at a tear-filled news conference, he confessed. Not only was the underwear picture the congressman's, he did indeed send it to the college student. And she was not the only recipient of his career-destroying cyber chatter.

A forty-year-old Las Vegas blackjack dealer announced that she had exchanged scores of sexting messages with Weiner, going public only after she was scorned. She told the scandal website *RadarOnline* that she contacted Weiner while he was busy denying he sent the underwear tweet. "I wanted him to know that I had no intention of coming forward and our past was going to be kept hush-hush," she said about the exchange of titillating notes between the two of them. When she failed to hear back from him, she went public. "He didn't return my messages," she said. "I discovered that Anthony is a bad man, and a liar." Twitter and Facebook account traffic can be archived, and the casino dealer disclosed traffic between her and the congressman. He folded and called the confessional news conference.

In August 2011, the sixteen-year-old former girlfriend of the German politician Christian von Boetticher was much more complimentary after he quit his job as a state legislator who was expected by his political party to become the next president of Schleswig-Holstein. "It was love at first sight," journalist Oliver Meyer at the Cologne *Express* reported she gushed, insisting their relationship was not just lust, but love. "We could talk for hours with each other," mused the schoolgirl, identified by the *Express* as Kathie S., calling von Boetticher " . . . a perfect man." And he was another man who couldn't keep his hands off the keyboard connected to his Facebook account. Soon after Representative Weiner cried at his New York news conference, the forty-year-old von Boetticher, who must have been so busy posting updates on his Facebook wall that he failed to pay attention to his New York colleague's mistakes, was weeping through his own resignation announcement.

The career of the Christian Democrat's rising star von Boetticher may well have survived fooling around with the teenager at the swanky Steigenberger Hotel in Düsseldorf. Sixteen is the legal age of consent in Germany, and German society doesn't suffer from America's puritanical instincts when it comes to judging the personal lives of public figures. What flummoxed his constituents was that he found his date (" . . . a very unusual love," he reported as he resigned) on Facebook, and that he spent an inordinate amount of his workday displaying his privileged life to the world via his wall postings: *Here I am at the beach! Here I am watching polo! Here I am drinking wine you can't afford!*

Don't bother trying to friend the former legislator on Facebook. Mr. von Boetticher—surprise!—finally seemed to get the point, and his account at last check is a void.

No question these affairs sold newspapers, and there's nothing wrong with all of us reading about still another politician falling from grace. Congressman Weiner's political suicide speech admitting that he was a smut messenger took place the same day that the former International Monetary Fund honcho Dominique Strauss-Kahn appeared in a New York courtroom facing charges of molesting a hotel chambermaid. The news that DSK was released on bail prompted another poetic *Post* headline: "FROG LEGS IT!"

Stories about the rich and famous are, of course, standard fodder for the popular press, especially when the stars of the stories engage in errant behavior and get busted for it. It's hard for many of us to believe that someone who enjoys a privileged lifestyle and is at the pinnacle of an illustrious career would risk it all for a few cheap thrills, let alone criminal behavior. And there is something viscerally satisfying (*Schadenfreude, ja?*) about witnessing such backslides. Years ago I applied for a reporting job with the tabloid *National Enquirer.* I spent two days at the scandal sheet's Lantana, Florida, headquarters and came away convinced I did not want to practice their style of journalism: stalking celebrities. But I did pay attention when one of the editors explained the paper's philosophy. "Every story," he told me, "should be about someone the reader either wishes he were or is glad he's not."

The ease with which we all now have access to innovations such as Twitter does not mean we ought to use these tools all the time, either to send messages or to receive them. I'm convinced that the vast majority of what is being flashed back and forth around the world is fatuous, or at least superfluous to our daily routines. We simply do not need to pay attention to the random thoughts of the billions of people on earth with access to the latest media technology. Now that just about everyone has access to the equivalent of a printing press and can be the equivalent of a publisher, those of us on the receiving end of what is being spewed forth must act as our own gatekeepers and editors; we must restrict what we bother consuming or we will be inundated by useless out-of-context factoids and the mindless opinions of masses of people hiding behind anonymous Internet facades.

That said, a commentator who identifies him- or herself only as "any mouse" responded on *The Huffington Post* to the fireworks around the Weiner story with advice worth considering. "Any mouse" commented on an article in which the student who received the underwear photograph complained that the *New York Post* reporter who managed to obtain an interview with her misrepresented himself. Still using a Twitter account (from which she tweeted, "I can't believe I'm back on Twitter!"), she complained, "You are everything that is wrong with journalism." The word from "any mouse" came fast. "ALL NEWS PEOPLE are subhuman. When will these 'innocent' victims realize that even being near anyone that might be in the 'news' (gossip) business is a humiliating, degrading experience." The anonymous poster offered more: "NEVER trust anyone in the 'news' business any farther than you can throw a bus, keeping in mind that they want you run over repeatedly by that bus." This invective brings to mind the devastating conclusion from critic Janet Malcolm who wasted the work ethics of us journalists as "morally indefensible." In her book *The Journalist and the Murderer*, Malcolm called all of us "a kind of confidence man, preying on people's vanity, ignorance, or loneliness, gaining their trust and betraying them without remorse." That brutal assessment is true at times, of course, but at the same time we perform a service necessary for a free society: we report the news.

If you choose to stay in the fast lane and succumb to the siren call of technological opportunities such as Twitter, at least know how the darn things work. Congressman Weiner's mistake was not only that it's usually a dumb idea to send pictures of yourself in your underwear to women you've never met. He erred in manipulating the technology. Unless because of some deep psychological flaw he was seeking to get caught with his pants down (so to speak), Weiner pushed the wrong buttons when he sent the fatal tweet. Perhaps he didn't understand the difference between what is called a *mention* (a public tweet mentioning a user, that must contain their username), a *reply* (another kind of public tweet, visible only to the followers of both sender and recipient, that must begin with the recipient's username), and a *message* (or what used to be a "direct message": a one-to-one, private message, not a tweet, that can only be sent to someone following you and that can only be seen by the recipient).

Confusing? You bet! Even for those—such as Weiner—who are supposedly skilled users of the latest technological developments.

There is no need to worry about these specific distinctions for keeping your world private. Would you trust the Twitter system even if you were convinced you knew how to send a private message to a specific follower of your account? Why should you trust the system? Even if Twitter managers are not spying on private messages, shouldn't we fear the system may fail and what you send as a private message may slip into the public sphere? Why should we feel compelled perpetually and immediately to yell our latest news to the rest of the world? We should filter our words with thought and time; that alone should save us from embarrassment and worse.

Back in the days of resisting the Vietnam War my colleagues and I always assumed our mail was opened and/or telephones were tapped. We adjusted our writing and speech accordingly, saving the secrets for personal meetings or communicating carefully using oblique codes. The apartment I shared in Moscow with other journalists during the transition period from the Soviet Union to the post-Communist era was equipped with an ominous warning sign on the handset of the telephone. It reminded us that we were not alone. "Speak only about the weather," demanded the note. Similar survival techniques still serve us, as journalists and otherwise, as Edward Snowden made clear when he leaked the NSA files detailing the U.S. government's universal domestic spying campaign.

If you say it into your mobile phone, expect to see it as a newspaper headline in the morning (or minutes later on Twitter!), if it's newsworthy (or just amusing). Assume your email is purloined along its path to your correspondents. Figure that your sweet nothings whispered over drinks in a dark barroom are being recorded for a scandal sheet by the bartender. Transparency may be the new objectivity for journalists. The corollary for the rest of the public is that privacy may only be possible if we keep ourselves off the digital grid: no *telefonini*, no Twitter, no email, no web surfing, no Skype, no Facebook. And there are old-school pre-digital lessons to remember: letters you send through the post may be scrutinized, that bartender may be taking notes about what you say. "Loose lips sink ships," read the World War II posters. Maybe an easier tactic than looking over your shoulder with perpetual paranoia is to follow Bob Dylan's old maxim, "If you ain't got nothin', you got nothin' to lose."

Of course while we self police our media intake, there's nothing wrong with enjoying a scurrilous story. As that *National Enquirer* editor taught me: we all like to read about someone else's sleaze once in a while, especially when their actions are so stupid it reinforces our self-righteous beliefs that we're too smart to make such mistakes. The instant nature of Twitter, the medium he was addicted to, both attracted and defeated Congressman Anthony Weiner (and defeated him a second time when the "rehabilitated" Wiener ran for New York City mayor in 2013 despite his continuing reckless tweets). Were he limited to communicating with his public via fountain pen on personal stationery sent through the post, would he have still made his foolish mistakes? Probably not. The laborious action of handwriting usually includes an almost automatic proofreading of a letter's content before it is sealed in an envelope. An email or a tweet or a Facebook post, like a comment on a website, are much more likely to be entered on a keyboard in a hurry and immediately sent into that pixilated world where they live on forever. Unlike thoughtless words written in ink on paper, you can't throw your tweets in a roaring fire and destroy them.

The Slow News rule is to suspect and expect that all forms of media are mass media.

Rule 21: Seek news that does not require batteries

A corollary to filtering the onslaught of nonstop incoming news-like information is to spend time with stories that interest you and you believe are important to your life. That may seem like a simplistic assignment, but the twenty-four-hour news cycle can overwhelm us with unnecessary information. We need to learn how to glance at the curriculum of new material endlessly generated, cull that which interests us, and jettison the rest.

There are some venues and some circumstances where the new and instantaneous media just don't work as well as the old and slow varieties.

Not long ago, I was on an American Airlines flight home and as it crossed the Sierra Nevada and began its descent toward the San Francisco International Airport, the stewardess made the usual announcement. "Please shut off all electronic devices," she said, and then added a litany of what she meant. "Computers, iPods, Gameboys, Kindles. Anything with an on-off switch." It was the first time I heard the Kindle—called a "wireless reading device" by its maker, Amazon—mentioned as something with the potential to interfere with aircraft navigation systems. I glanced out the window at the snow-capped peaks, looked ahead to the verdant Central Valley, checked my seat belt, and returned to the well-worn Sonoma County public library paperback copy of *Lucky Jim* that I had been reading since we left Dallas. The Kingsley Amis parody of academia written back in 1953 still resonates well in the twenty-first century, no batteries required, and with no prohibition on reading below twenty thousand feet.

I'm an author. I write books for a living. But if you choose the electronic version of one of my books—or any book—you'll miss more than the opportunity to read during take-off and landing. If you carry *Lucky Jim* and its ominous Edward Gorey cover illustration, it's bound to start conversations with passersby, as may any other book printed with ink on paper. No one knows what you're reading when you close the ebook on your iPad or shut off your Kindle. All that shows is a nondescript plastic box that advertises you as a relatively early adopter of new technology.

That anonymity may serve you well if your tastes in reading material tend toward pornography or how-to books on bomb making. But I wager most of us enjoy the impromptu conversations that start with a glance at a book cover.

When I was on that flight to San Francisco, *Lucky Jim* was not yet available on Kindle, although Amazon was offering 78 used copies of the Penguin paperback edition for as little as ninety cents each. The Kindle is a grand new tool, but it's no book. The same is true for digital versions of the daily news—they can be mighty convenient and useful, but they ain't newspapers.

There's nothing wrong with reading the *Washington Post* or the *San Francisco Chronicle* on your iPad. But it's easier to skim over the news when it comes delivered on an electronic tablet and harder to digest it. The digital devices become more sophisticated with each of their generations. Sure you can save stories from periodicals and share them with friends and colleagues. You can study reporters' primary sources via all sorts of immediate links. I can take notes on my iPad while I'm reading various published works. With a click you can jump to another resource and look up a word you don't know or fill in a historical fact you forgot or never learned. No need to bother yourself with a trip to the library, especially if it's the middle of the night and you simply must research a concept you fail to understand at that very moment. But, usually, what's the rush? This I-can-find-that-out-now attitude is exacerbating our shrinking attention spans and diluting our memories.

The world of the Kindle and iPad and their siblings is magic, but it needs to be used sparingly. Paper is a technology that can last centuries. Check out a Gutenberg Bible, for just one example; forty-eight copies are still known to exist, though only twenty-one are complete. But digital devices show us again and again that the information packed into them is perishable because of their ever-changing standards. How many floppy disks are cluttering your basement, and have you tried to read one on your iPad? We early adopters race to embrace the latest innovations often oblivious to what that means when we try to access work saved on now-archaic devices. What about the various documents you created on your first computers; did you recover all of them each time you graduated to a new machine? We lose love letters when we change email accounts. Do you worry that Amazon is capable of erasing words from that Kindle if it decides to ban or censor a book? It happened—hard to believe—with, of all books, *1984* by George Orwell, for example. Yet the trusty old books you and your family bought are resting in your home library, just waiting for you to return to them (after you go jogging, playing a cassette on your Walkman).

You can't mark stories up with marginalia notes in your own distinct handwriting that lasts on yellowing pages for posterity when you read *Moby Dick* on a Kindle. You can't tear out newspaper stories from an iPad to save them for further study or to stick them up on your refrigerator door for repeated reference by you and your family.

The Slow News rule is: Don't abandon the tried and true just because something flashier is sparkling in the showroom windows. Balance the digital magic with media that don't need batteries.

Rule 22: Don't become a news junkie

It is impossible to know all the news, all the time—no matter what the all-news radio stations claim. Take a break from what my news reporter colleague David McQueen calls, "The dismal details of the daily downer." Read a novel. Play your guitar. Bake a pie.

Another tactic is to excise a medium from your life. We really do not need to stay connected to everything all the time. If you feel you must keep your Facebook fix, consider dumping your Twitter account. If you cannot imagine a day without talk radio, skip the television chat shows. I offer myself as an example: I've not watched television in my home since the mid-1980s. Do not get me wrong. I am not an evangelist here preaching that you ought to shut off your TV. I'm just saying that it makes sense to me for us all to consider reducing the number of media devices we hook up to each day.

Here's what happened to me regarding television. When I was a child my parents decided that there would be no TV in our 1950s household. As I write this I realize I cannot remember ever discussing with them their rationale for keeping the tube out of the house. I imagine from these years later that they considered it a conduit of lowbrow culture (not that I much disagree, even today). Please excuse my not-so-latent elitism, but I think a healthy dose of elitism is just what the doctor should order, thank you very much. Our home—in Wisconsin in those days—was a European-American mélange, filled with books and the latest Hi-Fi equipment (reel-to-reel tape players and LP turntables back then) for playing fine recorded music. Stacked with the Beethoven and the Mozart were Jelly Roll Morton's jazz albums and recordings of the Army-McCarthy hearings. On Thursdays the cellist, violist, and other violinist came over and they and my father spent the evening filling the house with the sounds of their quartet. We drew pictures together, my mother cooked our dinners from scratch, and on Sunday nights we really did gather around the radio to listen to Jack Benny and Groucho Marx.

Not that I have a history free of television. During a nasty bout of what I recall was called the Asian flu—when the whole family was feeling miserable—we rented a TV set for about a week. And I used to run across the street to Jackie Lawton's house on Saturday mornings and watch *Sky King*. But I am not television literate. My popular culture references from that period of Americana are minimal.

Fast forward to the late 1960s. I was living on my own just north of San Francisco in what was still the Portuguese fishing village of Sausalito, filled with artists and tourists. I bought a television set and I became a television addict. This was in the days before cable television, in the days before satellite television, and of course well before TV shows were available on the still-to-be-created Internet. No YouTube then. All television came to us transmitted over the air. Where I lived in Sausalito the signal from San Francisco stations was blocked by the majestic hills of the Marin County headlands just north of the Golden Gate Bridge. But stations from California's capital city, Sacramento, drifted through the Coast Range, and I learned that if I affixed a square of aluminum foil to the antennae of my tiny portable TV I could receive shows from the three networks of the era—NBC, CBS, and ABC—more or less. The sound was not always clear and the pictures came with shadows and snow. But it was television, and I watched and watched, and I watched some more.

Fast forward again, and my brain is undoubtedly addled by years of happy talk newscasts, Johnny Carson *Tonight* shows, and endless sitcoms. I walked into the house one day and my young son was home from school on a gorgeous sunny day mesmerized in front of the television watching reruns of *Car 54, Where Are You?* on the Nickelodeon channel. I lobbied the family and won: we dumped the TV in favor of living a real life. And these many years later there still is no television in our household.

Of course I see TV shows periodically. When I am on the road I often turn on the sets in hotels to observe CNN, the BBC, and Fox News. I periodically check out specific shows that intrigue me, watching excerpts that I download from their websites or find on YouTube. *The Daily Show* is one of my favorites, particularly since Jon Stewart interviewed me about my butterfly book (and sales soared!). I know the lure and value of TV. I just choose to keep it out of my home because I fear—were it omnipresent—I would be seduced and do little else besides couch potato in front of the box being fed a steady stream of enticing commercials and mind-numbing programs.

As far as the news goes, I simply cannot spare the time to watch the TV version of the day's events. I invite you once again to time it yourself one day. Compare an hour with the TV news and an hour reading newspapers. You easily can get through a couple of quality newspapers in the same time it takes to watch one commercial-filled newscast. And, with a small number of exceptions, very few stories profit substantively from the pictures TV offers us. But try this other experiment yourself: turn on a TV newscast and shut your eyes. The pictures are almost always superfluous. Our imaginations service us well. That's why radio thrives.

So don't be a perpetual news junkie. The Slow News rule: Start the cure by getting rid of at least one medium. And television is a good choice for the ashcan of history.

Rule 23: Don't allow inelegant journalese to infect your personal lexicon

On the Larkspur ferry to San Francisco I overheard a conversation between two young women. The one with the peroxide hair, blue eye shadow, and matching nail polish enthusiastically told the other, "I met this gorgeous guy and we exchanged numbers! He's, like, a correctional officer in San Diego."

Excuse me, a *correctional officer*? How does a young woman, gossiping with another, manage to get tied up with a useless euphemism like correctional officer? What's happened to *jailer, screw, turnkey, keeper, warder* or—best of all—the plain and simple *prison guard*?

The blame for this diluted speech, at least in part, rests fairly and squarely on the news media. Listen to her conversation again with the right words: "I met this great guy and we exchanged numbers! He's, like, a prison guard in San Diego." It's fine, aside from the silly and useless fill word *like*; the only way the poor girl could end up with a soulless term like correctional officer is from watching too much TV and listening to too many radio newscasters. If a piece of steak got stuck in her throat during lunch later that day and she couldn't get enough air, she probably would have choked out, "Get me a medical technician, call for an emergency vehicle!" Once she got to the hospital, if it looked like she might not survive, she likely would have whispered to the nurse, "Call my next of kin!"

Broadcasters, with their perpetual influence on language, are themselves inordinately influenced by the shorthand and terminology that their sources use. Newscasters deal with the police and other government agencies daily, and phrases like *next of kin* get into broadcaster's vocabularies because that's what they hear from these authorities. A combination of laziness and a desire to sound official pushes too many radio and TV writers to say something like *next of kin* even though *relatives* is a much more natural word to pick. So fire trucks and ambulances become emergency vehicles, even though fire truck and ambulance take much less time to say and paint vivid word pictures. Emergency vehicle creates a vague image in the mind. It is too bad that tough and descriptive words are disappearing from the airwaves and being replaced with drab synonyms. But the real linguistic tragedy is that so many media consumers develop their vocabularies from what they hear on the radio, TV, and their favorite Internet outlets (or, to a lesser extent, read in the newspapers).

Consequently, we're raising a generation, like the blond on the ferry, that finds it easier to say "sanitary landfill" instead of "dump" or "convenience store" instead of Seven-Eleven or Autogrill. The loss of strong and specific words from our daily speech homogenizes the texture of language and makes for boring storytelling. And that's basically what both news reporting and conversation is all about: storytelling. A good reporter takes complex issues and distills them for those of us not expert in the subject matter. If a news report is confusing, find another storyteller.

The Slow News rule: Don't let the words of hack writers infect and degrade your personal lexicon.

Rule 24: Keep an eye out for corrections

If you still read newspapers in their ink-on-newsprint version, make the effort of reading the back end of front-page stories. Often juicy details are buried far from the lead paragraph. So are corrections.

George Kakaletris is a good example. He was from the Chicago suburb Palos Hills, and spent a couple of days in the media spotlight during the Gulf War back in 1991, telling his horrific war stories as a just-returned Army reservist. The stories were great copy: parachuting behind enemy lines, wounded severely in hand-to-hand combat. Kakaletris spun his yarn from the comfort of his family's living room, his leg bound in a no-fooling cast, one eye covered with a pirate's patch. The details were sexy: full of attacking Iraqis with knives and bayonets, a battlefield alive with rifle fire and exploding grenades.

Kakaletris got the fifteen minutes of fame he was looking for and that Andy Warhol promised is available to all of us at least once. Reporters jumped all over the story and editors rushed it onto the air and into print.

Probably the *Chicago Tribune* was the most embarrassed. Two days after its hero story, the *Tribune* printed a follow-up, this time reporting that, contrary to its earlier interview with Kakaletris, the Army had no records of the man serving since his discharge in 1987. Then came the most telling line in the *Tribune* correction. "In preparing its story," confessed the paper, "the *Tribune* made no attempt to confirm Kakaletris' story with the Army or with other independent sources." Incredible—the paper made no attempt to confirm the story with independent sources—but, unfortunately, not unusual.

Journalist and designer Mario Garcia tries to get us to read past the jump. He redesigns newspapers worldwide; *The Wall Street Journal* and *Die Zeit* are examples of his clients. I spoke with him about slow media, like newspapers, surviving the digital revolution, and he was sanguine about the future of print. "I am a firm believer that newspapers will always be around," he told me. "You have to realize that every time a new medium comes in there are rumors that another medium will disappear. In the late

1800s, when newspapers first appeared, there were articles written about the end of the book. Who would read a book when you can actually have something to read fresh every morning? When radio appeared, it was going to displace newspapers. Television was going to displace radio. No medium replaces another medium."

But in the current era, it's more difficult for Garcia and his clients to convince Americans than Europeans to read past the jump. "In Europe there's more of a loyal readership for newspapers. Readers are more tuned into newspapers." His research shows that Europeans spend more time with a paper than their American counterparts. "An average newspaper in any region of Europe will devote a great deal of ink and paper, sometimes without advertising, to literature and literary affairs." The reason is not necessarily that Europeans are more interested in books; it's business. "American newspapers are more commercial. Advertising doesn't like those pages too much. You don't have a lot of advertisers knocking on your doors to advertise in a literary section. I think newspapers abandoned the notion of being literary kinds of publications in the early twentieth century in the United States."

The Slow News rule: Read past the jump, click past the headlines, and find the juicy details, the corrections, and the explanations.

Rule 25: Romanticize journalism (some of the time)

How might the news you are consuming today—and the manner in which it is presented—affect you and others?

Watch the film *The Front Page* as a reminder of how much fun the newspaper business can be for reporters and readers, and what an addiction it can be. Read the Evelyn Waugh book *Scoop* to enjoy a parody of foreign correspondents, and for a look at the newspaper business that resonates with the 2011 UK phone-hacking crimes. Go to see the movie or the play *Talk Radio* for a lesson in the dangers of screaming at the radio audience. See the movies *The Soloist* and *The Fisher King* to learn just how influential reporters and radio performers can be even on those who don't bother to read their writing or listen to their shows. In *The Soloist* a dedicated *Los Angeles Times* reporter tries to rescue a derelict concert cellist he meets when he's combing the streets of L.A. looking for copy for his newspaper column. The cellist influences and changes the reporter at least as much as the reporter and his coverage of the cellist influence the homeless musician. The same is true in the *The Fisher King*; the film follows an arrogant radio announcer who comes to terms with the potency of the medium and his own vacuous broadcasting act.

I hope no one interprets my Slow News Movement as a campaign to turn us into news ostriches, sticking our heads in the media sand and ignoring the traumas that surround and plague us. On the contrary, the Slow News Rules outlined here are designed to give us a breather from the repetitive, superficial, and unimportant dump-truck loads of information that can inundate us if we're not highly selective about our news media intake. The perpetual onslaught of often-useless information that we're subjected to moment by moment in today's hyper-mediated world leads to what my nephew Alex calls "induced attention deficit disorder." It's a great term. Our mobile phones ring nonstop with text messages, emails, news bulletins from our favorite newspapers and TV stations—and sometimes even with a phone call from a friend who wants to talk with us so we can hear each other's voices. Too often we think we do not have the time to study a news story and figure out what would be a constructive reaction to it. The truth is we've got plenty of time for that editing work. We just must engage in some good old-fashioned mindfulness and shut off the excessive news media noise.

Romanticizing journalism can help. Think about swashbuckling reporters dashing around the world and taking risks just to bring us critical news dispatches. We owe their work the attention it deserves, just as we owe ourselves relief from the filler parading as news and being foisted on us day and night.

Consider the words of William Randolph Hearst's star foreign correspondent H. R. Knickerbocker. "Whenever you see hundreds of thousands of sane people trying to get out of a place, and a little bunch of madmen struggling to get in, you know the latter are newspapermen."

The Slow News rule: There is no better work on the planet than being a journalist. As my friend and colleague Markos Kounalakis reminds me, "We journalists are sentenced to lifelong learning." Not a bad fate.

Rule 26: Become a news reporter for a day

What is a journalist? Who is a journalist? The answer is remarkably simple: a journalist is anyone who experiences and reports the news. Though we have seen in Rule 7 that this is not the case all over the world, we maintain no government licensing of journalists in the United States. There is no professional organization anointing those of us who chose to practice journalism. The lack of such restrictions is integral to the establishment of a thriving free press. Even in those countries where access to the journalism profession is restricted, there often are alternative options for working as an informal reporter. Any of us can be journalists whenever we want to make that career decision. All we have to do is find an audience. To operate in any other manner would make a travesty of the concept of a free press.

I've always considered bartenders, barbers, and taxi drivers to be among our most influential journalists. They are constantly witnessing and interpreting the news, then they proceed to analyze it for their customers as an extra service.

But we don't need to wait until someone else reports the news to interpret it and analyze it. Anyone can decide to be a journalist, if only for one story. You may not succeed. You may even get hated, hurt, arrested, or worse. But we journalists take those risks every time we leave the house in our trademark trench coats and fedoras. Whether it is a local problem in your own hometown or an international crisis, consider the possibility of reporting it yourself.

Maybe you suspect corruption in your city's government. Perhaps you figure a garbage-collecting company received the contract to pick up the city's trash because of illegal contributions to the mayor's campaign. Maybe you have a source in the mayor's office and he hinted at the scandal after joining you for a few drinks at your favorite bar. How would you go about pursuing that story? Maybe it was nothing but a drunk's fantasy. But what if it were true, you established its veracity, publicized what you learned, named your initial source, and your friend was fired—or worse?

How about the Arab Spring in Egypt and its deterioration into civil strife and a military coup? What if you happened to be vacationing or on a business trip in Cairo when the crowds began assembling in Tahrir Square? You could have decided to be a journalist instead of rushing to the airport for the first flight home. You could have stayed up night after night in Tahrir, interviewing soldiers and protestors and passersby. But when thugs attacked the crowd, would you have had advance warning from one of your sources? Would you have thought to hire a local fixer who could have sensed the fast change in atmosphere and spirited you from the advancing danger before you were trapped? How would you have sent your reports to the world when Internet and mobile phone service were shut down by the collapsing Mubarak government?

All ramifications to consider if you decide to play my game: Journalist for a Day.

In fact, several years ago I designed just such a game. Not long after the Dutch company Endemol developed the reality television show *Big Brother*, it occurred to me that there may well be a hit reality TV show based on foreign correspondents. So I developed a treatment I thought was viable.

I envisioned a panel of contestants facing a live audience. Each of the contestants would have been vetted by producers to make sure that they were available to go anywhere in the world for a week. They would need to be healthy, not (too) crazy, and relatively well informed about world current events. The show host would be an effervescent character, along the lines of *Britain's Got Talent* presenter Simon Cowell. The panel of contestants would field questions about a specific breaking world news story. Examples from the relatively recent past would be stories like the Japanese earthquake-tsunami-nuclear power plant meltdown or the trapped Chilean miners or the prolonged crises in the Middle East. Questions would be fired at the contestants about the news of the week. The one who provided the most correct answers would be the winner, and the prize would be the opportunity to go report a story. In the treatment I wrote, the winner would leave immediately for the site of the story; I figured on a dramatic departure via a helicopter jump from the TV studio to the closest airport. A professional film crew and an experienced field producer would accompany the amateur journalist. The lucky winner would spend a week on the front lines of a war, at a natural disaster, in the midst of a famine—whatever the lead international story of the week might be—and return to the reality TV show set a week later to talk about the experience and show the audience the resulting reportage.

I thought it was a smashing idea. But all the TV executives I presented it to shook their collective heads in dismay, thinking about the legal liabilities of creating a business based on that plan. ("Send quiz show contestants into war zones? Are you out of your mind?") My experiences trying to peddle my news reality TV show was a reminder to me of just how unusual the risks are that we journalists take for granted as part of our work routine. A dedicated journalist, I am convinced, is attracted to the profession for three good reasons: the potential to change the world, the opportunity to earn a living doing that, and endless adventure en route to those goals. It takes a special type to do this sort of work; plenty of passersby would prefer the role of passive voyeur.

The Slow News rule: Don't blame the messenger.

Rule 27: Be a news maker

My friend and colleague Wes "Scoop" Nisker used to end his radio newscasts, "If you don't like the news, go out and make some of your own." What a classic line that is: "go out and make some of your own." Another of the many bad side effects of the twenty-four-hour news cycle is its potential to encourage the populace to be passive. "All this stuff is happening," the news purveyors scream at us. "And more stuff is happening! And keep paying attention to us news reporters so that you don't miss the next things that are about to happen!" The news business relies on its customers consuming news, not making news. If we allow the constant babble of news—or worse, a news-like babble—to intimidate us into believing there is nothing we can do to effect change, that news and more news is just going to happen to us, we deserve what we get.

In the late 1970s the fictional newscaster Howard Beale in the movie *Network* escaped from character, turned to his audience, and ordered them to yell from their windows, "I'm as mad as Hell, and I'm not going to take it any more." Such a yell would be a start, the beginning of "go out and make some of your own." But Scoop's assignment to his audience, at least as I interpreted it, was to do more than complain. He was reminding his audience daily that if what they heard him report was not the world they wanted to live in, it was up to them to change it.

The Slow News rule is stolen verbatim from Scoop: If you don't like the news, go out and make some of your own.

Rule 28: Exercise free speech

When I am home in America the elegant First Amendment to the United States Constitution protects my journalism. The simplicity of this first guarantee in our Bill of Rights is extraordinary: "Congress shall make no law respecting an establishment of religion, or prohibiting the free exercise thereof; or abridging the freedom of speech, or of the press; or the right of the people peaceably to assemble, and to petition the government for a redress of grievances."

That says it all. No law abridging freedom of speech or press. Of course there are times when laws or other rights come into conflict with the First Amendment. That's what the Supreme Court is for, to adjudicate such conflicts. Types of speech the Court has ruled the First Amendment does not protect are limited to an extremely short list (open to wide interpretation, case by case). Incitement is a good example. You do not have the right to yell fire in an American theater that is not burning. Engaging in fraud and defamation is not a legal right. Obscenity can be restricted, even if it is difficult to identify. Justice Potter Stewart famously defined obscenity with the personal, "I know it when I see it."

I tend to be a First Amendment absolutist. I'll take my chances with accommodating speech I find offensive, or even potentially dangerous, rather than risk a government empowered to censor me and my fellow citizens. I embrace the quote often attributed to Voltaire. "I disapprove of what you say, but I will fight to the death for your right to say it."

An example of a contemporary U.S. Supreme Court First Amendment ruling that gives free speech the benefit of the doubt was handed down in 2010. The Court—by an overwhelming majority—ruled that a law written to outlaw the buying and selling of so-called crush videos and videos of animal fights was unconstitutional. (Crush videos are the animal equivalent of snuff films. In them women, usually barefoot or wearing stiletto heels, crush the skulls of small animals.) The Justices, with an 8 to 1 vote, decided that even though the images portrayed may be pictures of illegal animal abuse, the law designed to curb the trafficking in such speech was intrusive. The law targeted anyone who "creates, sells or possesses a depiction of animal cruelty," and defined the depiction of animal cruelty as "a living animal is intentionally maimed, mutilated, tortured, wounded or killed." Much too broad, said the Court, expressing worry that it could be interpreted to prevent movies about hunting. Opponents of crush videos were advised by the Chief Justice to go back to Congress and work with lawmakers to draft a bill limited to purveyors of obvious abuse, such as the stiletto heels attacks.

Another difficult First Amendment ruling came when a group of American Nazi sympathizers, calling themselves the American Nazi Party, chose to demonstrate in Skokie, Illinois, home to a large number of Jewish Holocaust survivors. In 1978 the Supreme Court ruled such a parade, offensive as it would be, was protected speech.

Attitudes differ in locales around the world.

Don't try to buy and sell Hitler's tome *Mein Kampf* in his native Austria. Trade in the book is illegal. In Germany it's against the law to deny the Holocaust. Don't insult the king in Thailand unless you want to risk some serious prison time. In the spring of 2011 the Thailand-born naturalized American citizen Lerpong Wichaicommart was charged with posting such insults on the Internet. He was hauled off from his Thai home to jail and sat behind bars facing a twenty-two-year sentence.

The Washington-based think tank Freedom House (which is funded in part by the U.S. government) estimated in its 2013 survey that fewer than 15 percent of the world's population live in a country served by a free and independent press. But its report spotlighted Facebook, Twitter, and other mobile phone and Internet-based communication systems as conduits for free speech, citing their role in the Arab Spring uprisings. These borderless methods of keeping in touch continue to prove too resilient to fully control and completely suppress. Freedom House offered a top ten list it calls "worst of the worst" for press freedom. The villains are Belarus, Burma, Cuba, Equatorial Guinea, Eritrea, Iran, Libya, North Korea, Turkmenistan, and Uzbekistan. But the United States did not escape criticism. There is no federal shield law in my home country protecting journalists from being forced to disclose sources, while news coverage diversity is challenged by corporate ownership and a continuing collapse of advertising dollars. As for Italy, "it remained a regional outlier with its 'Partly Free' status, and registered a small score decline in 2010 due to increased government attempts to interfere with editorial policy at state-run broadcast outlets, particularly regarding coverage of scandals surrounding Prime Minister Silvio Berlusconi."

Reporters Without Borders, the Paris-based non-governmental international organization, also tracks press freedom. In first place it lists Finland, Iceland, Netherlands, Norway, Sweden, and Switzerland, lauding those European countries as "an example in the way they respect journalists and news media and protect them from judicial abuse." But the commentary to the organization's Press Freedom Index 2010 warns: "Thirteen of the EU's twenty-seven members are in the top twenty but some of the other fourteen are very low in the ranking. Italy is forty-ninth, Romania is fifty-second, and Greece and Bulgaria are tied at seventieth. The European Union is not a homogeneous whole as regards media freedom. On the contrary, the gap between good and bad performers continues to widen." Moreover, Reporters Without Borders notes that there was no progress in the several countries where they had pointed out problems. In Europe this is especially true for France and Italy, where in 2010 "violation of the protection of journalists' sources, the continuing concentration of media ownership, displays of contempt and impatience on the part of government officials towards journalists and their work, and judicial summonses" were registered. As a result, Italy ranks alongside El Salvador and Burkina Faso. France performs slightly better, but with a negative trend.

Gangsters outside of government impede press freedom. A prime example is just south of the California border. In Mexico drug-trafficking cartels successfully (and understandably) intimidate reporters into self-censoring their work. "You love journalism, you love the pursuit of truth, you love to perform a civic service and inform your community. But you love your life more," an editor in the border state Tamaulipas told *Los Angeles Times* reporter Tracy Wilkinson in the summer of 2010. "We don't like the silence. But it's survival." No surprise: the editor requested anonymity. The

Committee to Protect Journalists, a New York-headquartered independent organization founded by American foreign correspondents, counted thirty journalists murdered since former Mexican President Calderón took office vowing to break the narcotic cartels operating in his country. Its 2010 report noted that during the year "journalists were assaulted, kidnapped, or forced into exile, while media outlets were targeted by bomb attacks, making Mexico one of the world's deadliest places for the press."

Again from the First Amendment: "Congress shall make no law respecting an establishment of religion, or prohibiting the free exercise thereof; or abridging the freedom of speech, or of the press; or the right of the people peaceably to assemble, and to petition the government for a redress of grievances."

We Americans are not alone. Various governments offer similar guarantees to their citizens. Some are sincere, some become ironic when ignored, and still others were just empty words on paper. Yet free speech everywhere is and always has been an individual choice. No one can prevent any of us from saying whatever we wish to say. We may suffer after we exercise uncensored expression, but governments and other adversaries cannot prevent us from speaking out. They can only attempt to intimidate us into keeping quiet.

The Slow News rule is: Speak freely.

Rule 29: That Kodak moment is just a memory

Fast news is polluting our personal lifestyles and experiences.

In Barcelona for a conference, I went sightseeing up on the mountain overlooking the city, *El Tibidabo*. I watched hypermediated tourists not look at the sweeping view of the city and the sea, not look at the Basilica, not look at the *El Tibidabo* amusement park rides, not even look at their friends—in real time and real life. Most of the tourists I watched up on the mountainside were immediately mediating their experiences via their iPhones and their iPads, seeing the sights for the first time—as soon as they climbed off the funicular—through their so-called mobile devices (not even through old-fashioned traditional digital cameras). And as soon as they made an image—still or moving—they looked at it, showed it to their fellow travelers, and, perhaps, flashed it elsewhere around the world. Using their eyes alone to experience the dramatic and inspiring locale was an afterthought, or just skipped. Capturing the image with digital memory was more important than experiencing what used to be called the Kodak Moment.

Make the picture; go get a hot dog and a Coke. The tourist's work is finished.

The loss is enormous because the view at *El Tibidabo* is not imprinted on the conscious and subconscious with the same permanence when it is seen through the iPhone as when it is experienced directly by the body and mind. The mediated view dilutes memory; the tourists I watched were counting on the iPhone's appropriately named memory chip to perform that job. And the mediated view is absent the ancillary inputs that make for rich personal experience when our lives are unmediated except by ourselves: the feel of the sun and the wind; the lizards and butterflies in our peripheral vision (out of the iPhone frame); the song birds; bits of overheard conversation.

Nothing wrong, of course, with snapping pictures. I want to go back to *El Tibidabo* and take some of my own up there. But first I visited the place unburdened by camera, just soaking it all up, without even the notebook I'm writing in now. It's dusk back down in the city, and I'm at a café recreating my day with pen on paper, convinced my memory of putting twenty cents into the electric candle machine at the Basilica is vivid precisely because I did not pose the scene for my iPhone (which I do not own).

We're mimicking TV news videographers in our personal lives, and we should stop it, or at least slow down the nonstop digital documenting. The mediated experience is now the norm. We're living in the iPhone, seeing our lives through the monitor, a monitor that allows us to take a picture of ourselves as we watch—in that so-called real time—that picture being made. An instant iPhone self portrait seen as it is snapped memorializes a different type of moment than a picture posed for later viewing.

Back in the old days of photography, when it could take as long as an hour (!) for Fotomat to develop snapshots from the cartridge in your Instamatic, my father printed his own work in the darkroom of his studio. A sign on the door warned, "This is a darkroom. Don't open the door—you'll let out all the dark!" Living a perpetually mediated personal life makes it less likely we'll encounter the mysteries of dark rooms.

The Slow News rule is: Avoid media obstacles that interfere with a spontaneous life.

"My woman done left me, ran off with my best friend. Well, my woman done left me, said she ran off with my best friend. Details are sketchy at this time, so let's go to Jennifer Diaz standing by in Washington."

Reprinted from *The New Yorker*, with permission.

Join My Slow News Movement

It's time to launch the Slow News Movement (our motto: "Yesterday's News Tomorrow"). It rarely is important to be the first to know about a breaking news story. Break the habit of lusting after relatively unimportant and superficial news just because it's easily available.

I'm back where I started at the beginning of this book, writing— slowly—by hand. My laptop is stashed at my office. I left my mobile phone in my old Volvo. My iPad is shut off. My notebook is resting on my lap and this time, instead of writing with my trusty Staedtler Mars Lumograph 100, I'm using my Mont Blanc Meisterstück. And instead of a café I'm sitting this late afternoon in a bar: Luckey's Club Cigar Store is the name of the place. It's just down the street from where I teach at the University of Oregon, in downtown Eugene. I'm sipping a local beer, Double D Blonde it's called, brewed across the Willamette River in Springfield. In the glow of the bar's neon signs I can see well enough to scribble. I'm watching the bartender and his woman friend play a slow and friendly game of pool. I'm listening to the bar talk.

"My connection with Christ is supernatural," says a patron in a large voice from the far side of the barroom. "Christ and the Grateful Dead."

It feels like an ideal locale to think about my Slow News Movement.

The Sunday newspaper lies unread on my kitchen table. I'll get to it later today or tomorrow. There's no hurry.

I bought the Mont Blanc pen as a present for myself duty free on a Lufthansa flight from Ankara back to my home in Berlin (another *zweite Heimat*) after covering the 1988 earthquake in Armenia. I had rushed to the Turkey-Armenia border to report the story. Nothing wrong with that. Journalists getting word out to the world about the devastation in Yerevan undoubtedly stimulated donors to aid the Armenian victims fast. It was especially important to spotlight that disaster since the expiring Soviet Union was overwhelmed by the rescue and recovery crisis.

But the case I've been making in these pages is that most news can wait.

So I invite you to join my Slow News Movement. There are no criteria for membership other than a desire to control the news in your life. There is no initiation ceremony. There are no dues in this club, and there are no membership rules. We don't meet in a clubhouse; in fact we don't meet. There is no secret handshake or loyalty oath.

Groucho Marx famously proclaimed, "I wouldn't join any club that would have me as a member." My Slow News Movement more closely resembles anarchy than a social club. There are as many Slow News Movement tactics as there are Slow News Movement members. The only real tenet is to self mediate rather than succumb to media saturation. Find a Luckey's Club Cigar Store of your own, I suggest, and order a beer. Watch a game of pool—or better, play one. Slip some coins into the jukebox and punch up a favorite song—as long as it isn't the Beatles singing, "I read the news today. Oh, boy!"

The last Slow News rule: Let's take back the news cycle and define for ourselves what constitutes news we need to know and when we want to know about it.

Notes

Rule 1

1. Tiziano Terzani, *A Fortune-teller Told Me: Earthbound Travels in the Far East*, Three Rivers Press, 2002, pp. 46-47.
2. The Eugene (Oregon) *Register-Guard*, February 26, 2011, p. A2.
3. The BBC Editorial Guidelines can be consulted online at this address: www.bbc.co.uk/editorialguidelines/guidelines/
4. Edith Efron, "Why Speech on Television Is Not Really Free," TV Guide, April 11, 1964, p. 7.

Rule 2

1. Elisabeth Bumiller, "Raid Account, Hastily Told, Proves Fluid," *New York Times*, May 6, 2011, p. A12.
2. Gleick, James, "'Total Noise,' Only Louder," *New York* magazine, April 20, 2013.
3. Dowd, Maureen, "Lost in Space," *New York Times*, April 24, 2013, p. A23.

Rule 3

1. "Oslo: Bomb blast near Norway prime minister's office," *BBC News*, July 22, 2011 (www.bbc.co.uk/news/world-europe-14252515).
2. Penny Bender Fuchs, "Jumping to Conclusions in Oklahoma City?" *American Journalism Review*, June 1995 (www.ajr.org/article.asp?id=1980).
3. Jack Shafer, "How To Read the Bin Laden Coverage." *Slate*, May 2, 2011 (www.slate.com/id/2292717/).

Rule 4

1. Pew Research Center for the People and the Press, "Limbaugh Holds onto his Niche— Conservative Men," February 3, 2009 (pewresearch.org/pubs/1102/limbaugh-audience-conservative-men).
2. Paul Farhi, "Limbaugh's Audience Size? It's Largely Up in the Air," *The Washington Post*, March 7, 2009 (www.washingtonpost.com/wp-dyn/content/article/2009/03/06/AR2009030603435.html).
3. Sean Easter, "Limbaugh Asks, 'How Can America Be Islamophobic? We Elected Obama, Didn't We?'" *mediamatters.org*, August 25, 2010 (mediamatters.org/limbaughwire/2010/08/25#0046).
4. Ned Resnikoff, "Limbaugh: 'You can either have Obama and the Democrats or America. You can't have both,'" *mediamatters.org*, September 27, 2010 (mediamatters.org/limbaughwire/2010/09/27#0035).
5. "Self-proclaimed civil rights leader Glenn Beck's history of racially charged rhetoric," *mediamatters.org*, August 26, 2010 (mediamatters.org/research/201008260006).
6. Amy Gardner, Krissah Thompson, and Philip Rucker, "Beck, Palin tell thousands to 'restore America,'" *The Washington Post,* August 29, 2010 (www.washingtonpost.com/wp-dyn/content/article/2010/08/28/AR2010082801106.html).
7. "Blacked out," *The Economist*, March 24, 2010 (www.economist.com/node/15766358).
8. Özlem Gezer and Anna Reimann, "'You Are Part of Germany, But Also Part of Our Great Turkey,'" *Spiegel Online International,* February 28, 2011 (www.spiegel.de/international/europe/0,1518,748070,00.html).

Rule 5
1. "America by the Numbers: Fun Facts from the 50 States," *Parade*, May 1, 2011.
2. Susan Palmer, "It's not nation's strip club capital," *Register Guard*, May 6, 2011 (www.registerguard.com/web/newslocalnews/26210940-41/springfield-parade-magazine-strip-amusing.html.csp).
3. www.guardian.co.uk/theguardian/series/correctionsandclarifications
4. online.wsj.com/article/Corrections.html?mod=WSJ_footer

Rule 6
1. Robert Fisk, "War In The Balkans: 'Once you kill people because you don't like what they say, you change the rules of war,'" *The Independent*, April 24, 1999 (www.independent.co.uk/news/war-in-the-balkans-once-you-kill-people-because-you-dont-like-what-they-say-you-change-the-rules-of-war-1089075.html).

Rule 7
1. Jim Rendon, "Dan Rather: Inside Mark Cuban's Gilded Cage," *Mother Jones*, March-April 2011 (motherjones.com/media/2011/02/dan-rather-reports-mark-cuban-hd-net?page=3).
2. Anne E. Kornblut, "Jay Carney, former journalist, is named White House press secretary," *The Washington Post*, January 27, 2011 (www.washingtonpost.com/wp-dyn/content/article/2011/01/27/AR2011012707601.html).
3. Bennett Roth, "Former Journalist Signs PR Contract With Bahrain," *Roll Call*, March 22, 2011 (www.rollcall.com/news/former_journalist_signs_pr_contract_with_bahrain-204281-1.html).
4. Winston Wood, "Parting Thoughts: Winston Wood," *Columbia Journalism Review*, August 4, 2008 (www.cjr.org/parting_thoughts/parting_thoughts_winston_wood.php).
5. Stephen Strasser, *Registering Reporters: How Licensing of Journalists Threatens Independent News Media*, Center for International Media Assistance, November 23, 2010 (http://cima.ned.org/publications/research-reports/registering-reporters-how-licensing-journalists-threatens-independent).
6. Jonathan Oosting, "Old, new media agree: Michigan lawmaker's proposal to license journalists a slippery slope," *Mlive.com*, June 1, 2010 (www.mlive.com/news/detroit/index.ssf/2010/06/old_new_media_agree_michigan_l.html).
7. From the film *The Front Page* directed by Billy Wilder, 1974.

Rule 8
1. "Times-Union tries hard to avoid conflicts of interest," *Times-Union*, January 19, 2003 (jacksonville.com/tu-online/stories/011903/opc_11503484.shtml).
2. Vilma Rinolfi and Domenico Paparella, "Renewal of national collective agreement for journalists", *Eironline*, June 1, 2009 (www.eurofound.europa.eu/eiro/2009/04/articles/it0904039i.htm).
3. Chris Ariens, "Bin Laden Killed: Fox News, CNN Speculation Mashup of Sunday Night's News," *TVNewser*, May 3, 2011 (www.mediabistro.com/tvnewser/bin-laden-killed-fox-news-cnn-speculation-mashup-of-sunday-nights-news_b64545).

Rule 9

1. Albin Krebs, "Truman Capote is Dead at 59; Novelist of Style and Clarity," *The New York Times*, August 28, 1984 (www.nytimes.com/books/97/12/28/home/capote-obit.html).
2. Marco Cattaneo, "Il ritorno della carboneria," *Made in Italy*, August 16, 2011 (cattaneo-lescienze.blogautore.espresso.repubblica.it/2011/08/16/il-ritorno-della-carboneria/)

Rule 10

1. Barack Obama, "'Meet the Press' transcript for Sept. 20, 2009," *NBC News* (www.msnbc.msn.com/id/32935603/ns/meet_the_press/page/2/).
2. David Sirota, "Addicted to fake outrage," *San Francisco Chronicle*, February 13, 2009 (www.sfgate.com/cgi-bin/article.cgi?f=/c/a/2009/02/12/EDMU15SUFP.DTL).
3. Pew Research Center for the People and the Press, "Public Knowledge of Current Affairs Little Changed by News and Information Revolutions," April 15, 2007 (people-press.org/report/319/public-knowledge-of-current-affairs-little-changed-by-news-and-information-revolutions).
4. Sarah Schewe, "US: Questions on the NYT Continuous News Desk," *editorsweblog.org*, August 13, 2008 (www.editorsweblog.org/newsrooms_and_journalism/2008/08/us_questions_on_the_nyt_continuous_news.php).
5. Ferruccio de Bortoli, "La lettera del direttore de Bortoli," *Corriere della Sera*, September 30, 2010 (www.corriere.it/economia/10_settembre_30/lettera-de-bortoli_2d41fc98-ccd0-11df-b9cd-00144f02aabe.shtml).
6. "Corriere della Sera, "Referendum, vincono i sì sull'accordo tra Cdr, direttore e azienda," *Affaritaliani.it*, Febuary 24, 2011 (affaritaliani.libero.it/mediatech/corriere_sera_accordo_cdr_direttore_azienda240211.html).

Rule 11

1. Fininvest Group, "Company Structure" (http://www.fininvest.it/en/group/company_structure).
2. Nicola Porro and Pippo Russo, "Berlusconi and Other Matters: the Era of Football-Politics," *Journal of Modern Italian Studies*, 5, 3, January 2001 (users.polisci.wisc.edu/schatzberg/ps616/Porro2001.pdf).
3. Bruce Orwall, "In Interview, Murdoch Defends News Corp.," *The Wall Street Journal*, July 14, 2011 (online.wsj.com/article/SB10001424052702304521304576446261304709284.html).
4. Jane Martinson, "Murdoch interview could have been tougher, admits WSJ special committee," *The Guardian*, July 25, 2011 (www.guardian.co.uk/media/2011/jul/25/murdoch-interview-could-have-been-tougher-wsj).
5. http://www.npr.org/blogs/thetwo-way/2013/08/16/212560519/ny-post-axes-headless-body-in-topless-bar-headline-writer
6. Darryl Bush, "A kiss for the road," *San Francisco Chronicle*, September 1, 2006 (www.sfgate.com/cgi-bin/article.cgi?f=/c/a/2006/09/01/MNGBLKTIDQ1.DTL).

Rule 12

1. "Chris Hedges Speaks on Osama bin Laden's Death," *Truthdig.org*, May 1, 2011 (www.truthdig.com/report/item/chris_hedges_speaks_on_osama_bin_ladens_death_20110502/).

2. Megan McArdle, " Out of Osama's Death, a Fake Quotation Is Born," *The Atlantic*, May 2, 2011 (www.theatlantic.com/national/archive/2011/05/out-of-osamas-death-a-fake-quotation-is-born/238220/).

Rule 13

1. "Texas tipster: Angels told me of mass grave site," *CBS News*, June 10, 2011 (www.cbsnews.com/stories/2011/06/10/national/main20070512.shtml).
2. Dane Schiller and Zain Shauk, "Psychic who sparked Liberty County search fears attention," *Houston Chronicle*, June 8, 2011 (www.chron.com/disp/story.mpl/metropolitan/7602111.html).
3. Trudeau, G. B., "My Shorts R Bunching. Thoughts?: The Tweets of Roland Hedley," Andrews McMeel, Kansas City, 2009, p. 4.
4. Deborah Campbell,"The Most Hated Name in News," *The Walrus*, October 2009, p. 53.

Rule 15

1. Thanks to graduate teaching fellow Lisa Rummler at the University of Oregon for her help surveying world newspapers and for her other research assistance with the Slow News project.
2. "Tsunami-hit firms expect business as usual in Hungary," *Budapest Times*, March 19, 2011 (www.budapesttimes.hu/index.php?option=com_content&task=view&id=17114&Itemid=163).
3. Ruchika Rai and Bhawna Gandhi, "Tsunami causes ripples in Gurgaon," *The Times of India*, March 13, 2011 (articles.timesofindia.indiatimes.com/2011-03-13/delhi/28685315_1_narita-airport-tsunami-earthquake).
4. Patrick McKenzie, "Let's keep the Japanese earthquake in perspective," *The Sydney Morning Herald*, March 16, 2011 (www.smh.com.au/opinion/lets-keep-the-japanese-earthquake-in-perspective-20110316-1bwd3.html).
5. "Fukushima's ripple effects on nuclear power in Canada," *The Globe and Mail*, April 7, 2011 (www.theglobeandmail.com/news/politics/fukushimas-ripple-effects-on-nuclear-power-in-canada/article1975874/page1/).
6. "Wen to visit Japan's disaster-hit areas," *China Daily*, May 13, 2011 (www.chinadaily.com.cn/china/2011-05/13/content_12509445.htm).
7. "Italy: Enel plans to push ahead building Italian nuclear plants," *Adnkronos*, March 15, 2011 (www.adnkronos.com/IGN/Aki/English/Business/Italy-Enel-plans-to-push-ahead-building-Italian-nuclear-plants_311791171070.html).
8. http://www.camera.it/_dati/leg16/lavori/odg/cam/allegati/20110117.htm

Rule 18

1. For example, see www.youtube.com/watch?v=3sGy5VFTPSg
2. Pier Luigi Pisa (edited by), "Basta viaggi noiosi: i finestrini dell'auto diventano tablet," *Repubblica TV*, July 21, luglio 2011 (tv.repubblica.it/tecno-e-scienze/basta-viaggi-noiosi-i-finestrini-dell-auto-diventano-tablet/73041/71322?pagefrom=1).
3. DVIDS, "In the Fight: Episode 51," May 27, 2011 (www.dvidshub.net/video/116425/fight-episode-51).
4. David Barstow and Robin Stein, "Under Bush, a New Age of Prepackaged TV News," *The New York Times*, March 13, 2005 (www.nytimes.com/2005/03/13/politics/13covert.html).

Rule 19

1. David Carr, "Why Twitter Will Endure," *The New York Times*, January 3, 2010 (www.nytimes.com/2010/01/03/weekinreview/03carr.html).
2. George Packer, "Stop the World," *The New Yorker*, January 29, 2010 (www.newyorker.com/online/blogs/georgepacker/2010/01/stop-the-world.html).
3. See the video posted on StageRightShow YouTube channel on July 18, 2010, at: www.youtube.com/watch?v=t_xCeItxbQY.
4. "Video Shows USDA Official Saying She Didn't Give 'Full Force' of Help to White Farmer," *FoxNews.com*, July 20, 2010 (www.foxnews.com/politics/2010/07/19/clip-shows-usda-official-admitting-withheld-help-white-farmer/).

Rule 20

1. Raymond Hernandez, "Lawmaker Denies Sending Suggestive Photo but Doesn't Rule Out It's of Him," *The New York Times*, June 1, 2011 (www.nytimes.com/2011/06/02/nyregion/weiner-denies-sending-photo-over-twitter-but-is-less-sure-of-its-origin.html).
2. Dylan Howard, "Weiner Sexting Partner Reveals Her Identity, Says: 'He Called Me On Congress Phone!'" *RadarOnline.com*, June 6, 2011 (www.radaronline.com/exclusives/2011/06/weiner-sexting-partner-reveals-her-identity-reveals-%E2%80%98he-called-me-congress-phone%E2%80%99).
3. Oliver Meyer, "Boettichers Ex-Freundin: „Christian wurde massiv unter Druck gesetzt,"'" *Express*, August 16, 2011 (www.express.de/news/politik-wirtschaft/boettichers-ex-freundin---christian-wurde-massiv-unter-druck-gesetzt-/-/2184/9539224/-/index.html).
4. Cristen Conger, "'Weinergate' reveals perils of tweeting in public eye," *DiscoveryNews*, June 3, 2011 (news.discovery.com/tech/tweeting-in-the-public-eye.html).
5. "Gennette Cordova: New York Post Reporter Lied To Me," *Huffington Post*, June 6, 2011 (www.huffingtonpost.com/2011/06/06/gennette-cordova-new-york-post_n_871721.html).
6. any mouse, *Huffington Post*, June 6, 2011 (www.huffingtonpost.com/social/any_mouse/gennette-cordova-new-york-post_n_871721_91455713.html).
7. Janet Malcolm, *The Journalist and the Murderer*, Vintage Press, New York, 1990, p. 3.
8. Lauren Dugan, "Learn a Lesson from Weiner: Get to Know the Difference Between DMs and Replies... Fast," *AllTwitter*, June 7, 2011 (www.mediabistro.com/alltwitter/learn-a-lesson-from-weiner-get-to-know-the-difference-between-dms-and-replies-fast_b9869).

Rule 21

1. Brad Stone, "Amazon Erases Orwell Books From Kindle," *The New York Times*, July 17, 2009 (www.nytimes.com/2009/07/18/technology/companies/18amazon.html).

Rule 24

1. "Army Contradicts Suburban Man's Gulf War Story," *Chicago Tribune*, March 5, 1991 (articles.chicagotribune.com/1991-03-05/news/9101200695_1_army-reserve-army-official-story).

Rule 28

1. Thomas Fuller, "American Arrested for Insulting Thai King," *The New York Times*, May 27, 2011 (www.nytimes.com/2011/05/28/world/asia/28thai.html).
2. http://www.freedomhouse.org/report-types/freedom-press
3. Freedom House, "Freedom of the Press," 2011 Booklet, p. 12.
4. Reporters Without Borders, "Press Freedom Index 2010. Europe falls from its pedestal, no respite in the dictatorships," 2011 (en.rsf.org/press-freedom-index-2010,1034.html).
5. Tracy Wilkinson, "Under threat from Mexican drug cartels, reporters go silent," *Los Angeles Times*, August 16, 2010 (articles.latimes.com/2010/aug/16/world/la-fg-mexico-narco-censorship-20100816).